Jesus and Addiction

Jesus and Addiction

. . .

A Prescription to Transform the Dysfunctional Church and Recover Authentic Christianity

Don Williams

Recovery Publications, Inc.
SAN DIEGO

Published by Recovery Publications, Inc.
1201 Knoxville Street, San Diego, CA 92110
(619) 275-1350

Library of Congress Cataloging-in-Publication Data

Williams, Don, 1937–
Jesus and addiction : a prescription to transform the dysfunctional
church and recover authentic Christianity / Don Williams.—1st ed.
p.   cm.
Includes bibliographical references.
ISBN 0-941405-20-6 (pbk.):
    1. Codependents—Religious life.   2. Addicts—Religious life.
    3. Codependency—Religious aspects—Christianity.   4. Compulsive
behavior—Religious aspects—Christianity.   5. Spirituality.   6. Church.
    I. Title.
BV4596.C57W55 1993
261.8'3229—dc20   92-37757
                                                              CIP

Scripture taken from the New American Standard Bible, © 1960, 1962, 1963, 1968,
1971, 1972, 1973, 1975, 1977 by The Lockman Foundation. Used by permission.

Excerpt from **Addiction and Grace** by Gerald G. May. Copyright © 1988 by
Gerald G. May. Reprinted by permission of HarperCollins Publishers.

"Saved" by Bob Dylan is used by permission of the author.

Excerpts from **Bradshaw On: The Family**, by John Bradshaw, copyright date
1988. Reprinted with the permission of the publishers, Health Communications,
Inc., Deerfield Beach, Florida.

Excerpts from **When Society Becomes an Addict** by Anne Wilson Schaef.
Copyright © 1987 by Anne Wilson Schaef. Reprinted by permission of
HarperCollins Publishers.

The Twelve Steps are reprinted with permission of Alcoholics Anonymous
World Services, Inc. Permission to reprint this material does not mean that AA
has reviewed or approved the contents of this publication, nor that AA agrees
with the views expressed herein. AA is a program of recovery from alcoholism
only—use of the Twelve Steps in connection with programs and activities
which are patterned after AA, but which address other problems, does not
imply otherwise.

Printed in the United States of America
First edition

10 9 8 7 6 5 4 3 2

For Kathryn

Acknowledgments

. . .

My gratitude goes to those who have shared their hearts and sufferings with me along the way. These include many who came off of Hollywood Boulevard years ago and taught me much about raw drug addiction as we lived and struggled together. Later, special friends and families in the San Diego area, whose names are omitted or changed for their protection, increased my knowledge and experience of the ravages of addiction.

I especially want to thank Dr. Francis and Judith MacNutt and Rena and George Larson of "Fishnet, Northeast" who have included my input in several healing conferences on addiction and codependency. I am also grateful to Owen Wickstrand for introducing me to John Bradshaw's writings and to John Wimber who welcomed me into the Vineyard Christian Fellowship and the congregation of the Coast Vineyard in San Diego which, through many trials, is growing with me into health as one vital part of the Church.

My special thanks also to Bob Manley of Recovery Publications for his constant encouragement and oversight of this project and to Jan Johnson, my editor, who taught me from her head and heart and made this a much better book.

Kathryn, my wife, stood by me throughout this project and gave up much of our personal time together so that I could finish my writing. She is a constant source of creative challenge and inspiration to me. My love for her is special, tested, and enduring. The strengths of this book are due to many people, the weaknesses are mine, and the glory is God's.

DON WILLIAMS
La Jolla, California

Contents

. . .

Introduction

Confronting Addiction: A Personal Journey

. . .

My thesis is simple: We live in an addictive culture that has helped to create a Church made up of addicted and codependent people. If we continue in our denial over this, like drug addicts we shall surely die. If we can break through this denial, then Jesus will set us free, and the Church will live again. We need to take a fresh look at how the surrounding addictive culture impacts us across denominational and theological lines. The time for the glorification of the decline of mainline churches has passed. Huge membership losses are not, as we had supposed, the elimination of deadwood. The addicted world is grinding up the Church, leaving little that is distinctive of her life.

My pilgrimage as a pastor has involved dealings with drug addicts and alcoholics as well as my own addictions and codependency. Through this journey I began to look at the Church with new eyes. Reading and reflecting about addictions helped me make sense of my own experience in the Church by placing it in a larger, addictive cultural context. I will share much of myself in the coming pages. I have not written about addictions in general or even solely for Christians recovering from their addictions; those fields are well covered. If you need more information about personal recovery, the notes at the end of the book can help you find your way.

This book *is* for and about pastors and laypeople who share responsibility for making the Church a part of the addictive system rather than God's intended instrument for redemptive recovery. Unfortunately, people can become addicted to religion and the Church. But, as from other addictions, they can recover. As individuals within the Church, Christians will then begin to see the recovery of the Church itself. People still need to repent of sin and be forgiven, but addiction needs to be healed. Jesus, who has come from the heart of God, is the healer and the cure for sin and addiction.

My awareness of the pervasive issue of addiction began when Al, a friend of mine, revealed to me that his daughter was a sex addict. By confronting her, he recognized his own addiction to work. (He was never home and was compulsive about making money and "doing the next deal.") He then realized that his own absentee father, a pastor, had set an example for him through his addiction to his church.

As we talked, I suddenly saw that I lived among twenty-eight thousand addicts in a wealthy California seaside community. These people had to be compulsive and obsessive just to make their mortgage payments, sustain their standard of living, and impress each other at gala benefits. On further reflection, I acknowledged that I knew very few healthy, functional families living in the community. No wonder I had become involved with so many kids on drugs. They were just continuing the unbroken chain of their parents' addictions. Little by little, the realization that people can be addicted on so many levels opened the door for me to come to terms with my own issues. I recognized that I was not simply a part of the solution; I was also part of the problem.

I had served on the staff of Hollywood Presbyterian Church during the Jesus Movement in the late 1960s. Through my ministry with college students, I found myself in contact with dropouts of the counterculture. I dealt with drag queens, runaways, unwed mothers, drug addicts, and a host of other wounded people from the streets. I quickly became totally preoccupied with their pain. As a result, I lost touch with my own feelings. Living in perpetual crisis, I did anything for the sake of those who had become the objects of my ministry. As my reputation grew in Christian circles, I realized I had let personal issues slide. I had become involved with Christian musicians who were achieving fame. But instead of confronting their "star" egos, I placated them because I needed them to further my own success. My outreach to street people was gaining public notice, and I thrived on that recognition. When the door to city hall opened, I was glad to walk right in. Political clout enhanced my image.

Meanwhile, my physical and emotional health deteriorated; I sat at the brink of a nervous breakdown. Even in that state there was no way that I would admit my addictions to adrenaline caused by crisis situations, caffeine, sugar (another addictive drug), my self-image as a "radical" Christian, and my many codependent relationships in the church where I served.

Later I would come to understand that I was unconsciously using my tumultuous life to fill an emptiness in my soul that only God could heal. But at that time I stuffed my ministry— little by little—into the void instead. The more I stuffed addictive behaviors into this painful void, the bigger it grew. It would not be filled. As my frantic activity consumed me, I became powerless over it. I was addicted to the point of complete physical and emotional exhaustion. To compound my condition, the Church fed my problem because it had become an addictive organization in its own right.

Eventually, I had to stop trying to fill my inner void. Instead I had to face my pain directly. What had caused this emptiness? Confronting this question, I reviewed my life, looking for clues.

I was born in 1937. I clearly remember my parents' anxiety when the announcement came over the radio that Pearl Harbor had been bombed. Like the rest of the world, we were caught up in events beyond our control. At four years of age I lost my dad's presence, apart from occasional visits, to the war. He returned in 1945, and the family made a slow adjustment to having him back. But for five years my father hadn't been there to play with me or pray with me. I had not had him to show me how to throw a football or to give me advice when I got beat up in my first fight.

Looking back on those years, I know that I felt rejected and abandoned because of my dad's departure. I know that he had no control over the situation, but how could a four-year-old understand this? Deep inside I had translated his actions to mean that I was not worthwhile enough for him to stay. Despite my mother's love and heroic spirit, during those years I missed and needed my dad.

As a result of my dad's wartime departure, rejection has been a core issue of my life. I have done almost anything to avoid it. Confrontation evokes acute anxiety in me; speaking the truth directly and risking the consequences creates fear. My early message lingers: "If you reject me, I must deserve rejection." I can easily be used and abused by people because I need to hold on to them regardless of the cost. If they leave I will be left with a hole that says, "I am worthless." How easy I found it to fill this hole with addictive substances, activities, and relationships.

In my dad's absence, my mom taught me to be a servant. I received strokes and rewards for helping others. Her motto was to leave the world a little better than she found it. When I applied this principle to myself, it was on top of an already diminished sense of my own value. I didn't want to risk her disapproval and lose her love as well as my dad's. Under her direction I sought value outside of myself. Not that this was all bad! I owe much of my servant's heart and leadership ability to her coaching. I was trained to meet the needs of others. I became *very* good at it.

Again and again, I've had people tell me, "Don, you're my best friend." I listen to them, hang out with them, invest my time in them, and care for their needs. And they trust me as a result. My reward from the friendships I accumulated was everyone's appreciation, approval, and dependency on me. Yet while I become their best friend, I've never had a best friend until very recently. As my wife Kathryn once said to me, "You can have a friend, but you can't be a true friend until you let people know your needs." The hardest words for me to speak are, "I need . . ." But I light up when someone else says, "I need . . ." What a setup for codependency.

No wonder I have been vulnerable to burnout and workaholism. My heart has cried out, "If I perform for you, if I gain your approval, then I will fill the emptiness inside and be able to love myself." But, humanly, my efforts are never enough. Only giving myself up to God's love is enough. But I've tried everything else rather than make this ultimate surrender.

Furthermore, much of my life has been lived on a feeling level outside of myself. My rich intellectual life was not matched by a rich emotional life. My parents' bouts with Christian Science left them and me in denial over negative thoughts or emotions. Anger, grief, and fear were unacceptable. Sex was treated with shame and silence. Sin, sickness, and death were illusions. Instead, my sister and I were to "think happy thoughts." Such control created half persons. Negative feelings existed, but they were pushed down.

In sum, my childhood, while immensely happy at times and secured by parents and a sister who genuinely loved me, was damaged. My dad's absence, my mom's denial of negative thoughts and emotions, and my search for complete value through meeting the needs of others created a sense of being lost to my own needs and emotions. This all resulted in an inner loneliness—what addiction expert John Bradshaw calls "the hole in the soul." This was a perfect setup that led me to become a servant of the Church and, conversely, to be abused by the Church I served. I became addicted to its life and ministry.

During the last few years, I have increasingly realized that the Church has been a breeding ground for my own and others' addictions. I progressed through seminary and ten years of ministry in Hollywood. Then, during a second pastorate in the Presbyterian church, I was abruptly fired by the elders. This traumatic experience prepared me for a new church. I finally felt at home in a small independent movement of churches called the Vineyard. Here I found my family at last with people I could not only work with but could trust and love unconditionally. Yet, after pastoring a new church for three years, all fell to shambles once again. My associate pastor and friend left abruptly in December 1990, without process or notice, which blew the church sky-high. Innuendo and gossip spread like cancer and fed the confusion and pain of the congregation. Over the next several months, scores of people followed this pastor, slowly bleeding the leadership, finances, and attendance.

To my horror, I could control none of this. At one point the board had to cut salaries. Later, they had to let another associate pastor go. As our church broke apart, I had to face myself and find God's hand in what had happened. My heart was broken and exposed. Unsettling questions came to mind. Why hadn't I confronted my former associate when I knew that our communication was strained and breaking down? Had I needed his acceptance so much that I couldn't risk being honest with him? Were my rejection and abandonment issues keeping me in denial and controlling my life? Had I developed a dependent relationship with him that had become addictive? Bluntly, God surfaced all of this because he wanted me to repent, be forgiven, and be set free.

I went into mild depression. It felt as if I were being hit again and again by parishioners. When would it ever stop? I could have become hardened at this point, but miraculously just the opposite took place. As my heart was broken, I became more tender and vulnerable than I had ever been. My friend Jay Hoehn was with me during this time, repeatedly demonstrating his unconditional love. Finally, I trusted him enough to blurt out words that shamed me, "I can't admit my needs to anyone, because I don't believe that anyone will meet my needs." The effect of my dad's absence was now laid bare. The sense of abandonment I experienced then had spread over my whole life. No wonder even my own wife, Kathryn, had such a hard time feeling needed by me.

Through the wrenching experience of a church split, the groundwork had been laid for me to admit my inadequacies and let people into my life in a new way. As I tried painfully to acknowledge my needs to others, I received love and care in return. With this experience came a new realization: I must be worth something because these people genuinely want to serve me and invest in my life. They see something in me that is worthwhile, even when I don't. Rather than running from my needs, they respond to my needs.

Forgiveness for those who had hurt me became a functional reality rather than a mere theological assertion. Through professional help, the communication logjam in my marriage began to break up. Kathryn and I started to know each other rather than simply bounce off of each other. This gave us a new closeness that grew rapidly. Paradoxically, acknowledging my negative emotions and letting them surface increased our intimacy as well. A few good arguments helped us get to our feelings and understand them. Often in the past, Kathryn would accuse me of being angry. With my mom's "happy thoughts" tape playing, I would immediately deny her accusation. But she was right. Now, with her sympathy and love, I am able to acknowledge the full range of my emotional life more and more. What a boon! At last, I am becoming real.

Presently I find growing within me a quiet sense of strength and a sense of who I am. These new feelings about myself are covered over less and less by the pious dodging or parental judgments that played like old tapes in my brain. Although I have carried a shame about my body and athletic failures for a lifetime, with the help of Kathryn I am beginning to accept my body as it is. I appreciate it as a gift—a good part of God's creation. I can now admit that I enjoy working out physically. I relish my sense of humor, even when others miss the delicious ironies that I see. I like the way my mind works; I enjoy both the order and creativity that spring up at times. I like the way I can make connections between ideas and burrow into the causes of things that are important to me. I like to fantasize and dream. I like the full range of my emotions, even the negative ones, which lead me to delight in the mercy and forgiveness of God when needed.

I can respond to my wife's longing for intimacy now that I understand the solitude that she has endured through most of our marriage. I realize that her loneliness in our relationship stems, in part, from my own alienation within myself. Now my shell is cracked and breaking.

With the help of my close friend Jay I am experiencing a new kind of relationship, knowing that he will not abandon me regardless of what he discovers about me or what happens to me. Little by little, I am able to take strength into other relationships as well.

If growth only comes through pain, then I am experiencing a growth spurt. This book reflects that growth, both in its analysis of the causes of our personal and collective agony, and in the solution offered in the gospel of God's free grace. Out of this grace will come a new relationship with Jesus, the only fully functional person. This discovery of the true Christ will renew our relationship with a new Church recovering from its dysfunctional and addictive behaviors. Finally, Christians will be able to disciple each other and bring each other into an authentically new life.

This newness can only come from brokenness. I wish there were some other way, but there isn't. "God is opposed to the proud, but gives grace to the humble" (1 Pet. 5:5).

Jesus says that if a grain of wheat does not die, it remains alone. This is our ultimate choice: loneliness or the death of our false self. But Jesus does not leave us in death. Now the hope comes thundering through. "If a grain of wheat dies, planted deeply into the soil, it will bear much fruit" (para. John 12:24). We long for this fruitfulness in our inner life. God has this full life for all of us.

Through our brokenness, God is on the move. It is that way for me, and it will be for you. But first, we need a clear analysis of our individual and collective problems. Addiction is rampant; the statistics and signs are everywhere. Yet, we have a God who is more radical than any diagnosis, and that is the good news. If we journey through both the pain and the healing together, I believe that neither you nor I will be the same again.

Part One

The Dysfunctional Church

. . .

Chapter 1

Naming Addiction in the Church

. . .

The news is in, and it's not good. Ninety-six percent of us come from unhealthy (dysfunctional) families. Most of us employed in the helping professions (counselors, pastors, doctors, psychologists, and social workers) are untreated codependents in addictive relationships. Over seventy-five million of us are touched directly by the disease of alcoholism alone. Eighty-two percent of all nurses are the oldest child of an alcoholic parent. Around 60 percent of all women and 50 percent of all men in this country have eating disorders.[1] The ultimate insight and insult to our egos has been given by psychiatrist Gerald May as he concludes, "I am not being flippant when I say that all of us suffer from addiction. Nor am I reducing the meaning of addiction. I mean in all truth that the psychological, neurological, and spiritual dynamics of full-fledged addiction are actively at work within every human being. . . . We are all addicts in every sense of the word."[2]

May means we have become psychologically attached to other people, processes, or substances that we use to alter our moods and fill the emptiness inside. This attachment actually changes brain patterns, programming us for continuing use and abuse. Since the mind or body quickly reaches a level of tolerance, we will need more and more of our addictive object to achieve a "high." Spiritually speaking, this is idolatry. Our addictions take the place of God, who should be the ultimate object of affection in our lives.

Behind Closed Doors

Pastors, as well as laypeople, are in crisis. They suffer from a range of addictions, including alcohol, prescription drugs, food, pornography, sex, and the very congregations they serve. This pastoral sickness is the Church's family secret, which we refuse to discuss. When congregations deny this problem, they expose their own sickness.

After graduating from seminary in the Midwest, a friend of mine found himself pastoring a well-known congregation in one of the wealthiest communities on the West Coast. Although appreciated by his congregation for his thoughtful sermons and commitment to social justice, his ministry was abruptly ended one night when a drunk parishioner invaded his board meeting and accused him of having an affair with her. As it turned out, this married pastor and family man also was carrying on extramarital affairs with several other women in the congregation. The matter was hushed up by his bishop, and after some legal maneuvering, he was quickly barred from professional ministry.

My friend's experience is no isolated case. *Newsweek* magazine recently published a story headlined, "When a Pastor Turns Seducer."[3] One of the article's case studies was about a forty-five-year-old married minister with fifteen years of service in the Lutheran Church. He had become a heavy drinker and had had sexual relations with sixteen women during his tenure. He described his activity as "authority rape." Shame finally led him to get help; he first gave up drinking and then found a therapy group where his condition improved over a period of time. His exposure by the women he had seduced resulted in his expulsion from the clergy. This is no extreme case. The Wisconsin Coalition on Sexual Misconduct found that 11 percent of all perpetrators were clerics, with 89 percent of their victims women.

Abuse and addiction aren't just a problem of the clergy. In a major congregation in San Francisco, a couple volunteered to handle its child care program. Happy to have this troublesome responsibility lifted, the Church entrusted sixty to seventy small children to them. The youngsters were then systematically sexually abused by this couple and their friends. Families became alerted as children began abusing each other. When the full horror came to light, the Church and its leadership were traumatized to the core.

There are countless incidents of alcohol and prescription drug addiction among the clergy and laity. Recognition of alcoholism as a sickness rather than a sin has allowed more pastors to "come out of the closet." Professional ministers often fall into substance abuse in order to lift, even for a moment, the burdens of their parishioners which, they have chosen to carry alone, to fill their personal emptiness.

I have also known elders and church leaders who could not face an important meeting without a few stiff drinks. A lay friend of mine, who has a successful evangelistic ministry, finally admitted that he had been addicted to drugs over much of his life and subsequently entered a thirty-day treatment program. Thankfully, alcoholism and drug addiction among the laity are finally being addressed. With the stigma of "demon rum" being lifted, Christ-centered Twelve-Step programs are appearing in many parishes.

Another alcoholic friend, and recent convert, confessed that his drinking was only a setup for satisfying his sexual promiscuity. Sex was his core addiction and the real reason for his barhopping. Again and again people have reported to me their shock at seeing elders and church leaders entering adult bookstores, picking up prostitutes, or cruising gay communities. Neither denial nor traditional moralizing over this darkness will help Christians who are in this kind of pain.

The most unrecognized addiction is workaholism. Christians justify this disease by attributing it to their religious calling and the demands for success that they believe those callings bring. Highly visible ministers produce torrents of sermons, books, and radio and television programs. They build new buildings, raise huge sums of money, hold endless committee meetings, chair expensive training seminars, jet here and there, and court powerful business leaders who can support their empires. They also set the standard for their humbler brothers and sisters.

As clergy live this lifestyle, their true emotions and their families are left in the lurch. Evenings at home are a luxury. As one abandoned minister's wife said to me regarding her absent husband, "How can I fight God?" Truer questions would have been, "How can I fight the Church?" or "How can I fight my husband's ego?"

Workaholic clergy necessarily attract and foster workaholic laity. Enamored by the value of "bigger is better," congregations feed into programs that become ends in and of themselves, often fueling the narcissism of their leaders. Authentic relationships and human failures are buried under the hype that keeps the money rolling in to feed the image of a successful congregation. Style rather than substance rules the Church in this media generation. No wonder a great emptiness, behind the glitter and glamour, is being felt by many Christians.

If most pastors and church leaders are workaholics, virtually all congregates are codependent. We help leaders to base their whole identities on the Church. As a result, we become enmeshed in a damaging cycle that makes us all Church addicts. The idea that pastors and lay leaders are addicted to the Church as a drunk is addicted to cheap wine is unthinkable. Nevertheless, for many leaders, the people of the parish serve as their drug. Ministers use congregations to alter their moods, determine their well-being (or lack of it), and fulfill their messianic fantasies. After all, aren't the clergy supposed to be consumed by their "higher calling"? Shouldn't they prove to the rest of us that "total commitment" to God is still possible? Aren't they supposed to be our surrogate parents, offering us the acceptance and nurture that we missed as children?

Parishioners often applaud and even mimic this self-destructive behavior. They too discover the "rush" or the "high" that being involved in codependent relationships can bring. As I have discovered, value and meaning can easily be found outside of ourselves. We meet our own addictive needs by meeting the needs of others. As a result, we serve the Church for ourselves. This is the hidden sickness of codependency. This is the ultimate selfishness that no one wants to see.

Addicted and codependent leaders build churches that become extensions of their own sickness and function as addictive organizations. As the disease progresses in the individual and is caught by the congregation, institutions behave more and more like a collective addict. It's not surprising the Church, across all denominational lines, is in spiritual crisis and statistical decline.

Quests to make the Church cater to society will be, at best, quick surface fixes with hollow cores. If we think that new leadership, increased funds, slick programs, and astute market research will restore our fortunes, we are dead wrong. Even a return to "traditional values" by rebuilding the "family altar" and returning prayer to the public schools will not heal us. The malaise that we face crosses denominational and theological boundaries. As in Noah's ark, all the different species in Christendom are riding out the storm together. Before any healing can take place, all Christians must face the sickness of addiction head-on. We must break through the first symptom, denial. By refusing to admit our addiction or codependency to the Church, we are only revealing the seriousness of our disease.

A Matter of Definitions

Although I didn't know it at the time, my addiction to processes and people in the Church followed the classic three-step definition of addiction:

1. Trying to please in order to gain pleasure and avoid pain.
2. Fearing the loss of pleasure, resulting in the repetition of reinforcing experiences.
3. Shutting down emotionally, rendering the individual incapable of experiencing the full range of human feelings.

Addictions begin because we want to experience pleasure and avoid pain. To do this, we attach ourselves to other people, behaviors, and things that make us feel good. Repetitive behavior reinforces such attachments. As a result we become preoccupied, obsessed, and then enslaved. Gerald May writes,

> For generations, psychologists thought that virtually all self-defeating behavior was caused by repression. I have now come to believe that addiction is a separate and even more self-defeating force that abuses our freedom and makes us do things we really do not want to do. While repression stifles desire, addiction attaches desire, bonds and enslaves the energy of desire to certain specific behaviors, things, or people. These objects of attachment then become preoccupations and obsessions; they come to rule our lives.[4]

This attachment to objects of desire may make us feel good, but soon it becomes a means of bondage. During the Jesus Movement I felt exhilarated by street ministry, campus riots, and the chance to help people in perpetual crisis. It was better than any drug-induced high. But I became trapped by my exhilaration, which almost killed me.

Psychologist Stanton Peele, in a pioneering study of addictions, notes that the addict is basically fearful. Peele writes, "Disbelieving his own adequacy, recoiling from challenge, the addict welcomes control from outside himself as the ideal state of affairs."[5] How, then, does this concept of addiction apply to ministers? Their fear of failure and subsequent abandonment and job loss results in their need to "people please." To them their questions easily become, "What does my church want? How can I make the congregation happy? How can I keep people coming?" The question should rather be, "What does God say my church needs?"

The shift may be subtle, but it's clear. Rather than being God focused, leadership easily becomes human focused and self focused. In a famous theological debate of the last generation, Paul Tillich asserted that the world asks the questions that the gospel then answers. Karl Barth replied that the world doesn't know the right questions to ask. This is to the point. In many churches functional authority has passed from Jesus to the people. When pastors continually ask what the official board wants or what the people want, they admit that control from the outside rather than the Spirit's direction on the inside is the ideal state of affairs. Rather than acting, the codependent leader spends his or her time reacting.

Beyond the need for pleasure and release from fear, Alice Miller observes that most of us have been set up for addiction by the verbal, physical, or sexual abuse we experienced as children. As a result we become detached from our feelings. We've been called names like "dumb," "stupid," "ugly," or "fat." We've been hit and spanked. In her words, we are "decent people who were once beaten."[6] Many have been sexually assaulted and molested. Today this includes 20 percent of all male children and more than 40 percent of all female children.

Such abuse means that many suffer from an emptiness caused by repressed childhood feelings involving a sense of powerlessness, personal violation, and ungrieved childhood losses. We've been raised in families where we weren't allowed to express how we thought and felt. This repression has been justified by what Miller calls "poisonous pedagogy," a misinterpretation of the fourth commandment to "honor your father and your mother." This commandment is taken to mean unquestioned submission from a weak and fearful child. Miller writes, "If he is prevented from reacting in his own way because the parents cannot tolerate his reactions (crying, sadness, rage) and forbid them . . . , then the child will learn to be silent."[7] This emotional shutdown is the root of a disintegrated personality. The destruction of the child's inner life results in "the psychic murder of the child."[8]

We are set up to become addicted; we are creatures who naturally seek pleasure and avoid pain. We are inherently fearful, needing to have our moods altered and welcoming outside control. We have been emotionally shut down by abusive parents who, themselves, were the victims of similar abuse. Our "inner child" wants to break out and explode as our addictions rush to fill this vacuum.

The Symptoms of Addiction

How then do we recognize the illness of addiction? The "Three Cs" provide a handy formula. First, there is the *craving*, or the need for a fix. We continually want our moods altered. Withdrawal of the mood-altering substance or process and the subsequent letdown only serves to reinforce our cravings. For example, an architect friend and elder in our congregation, experienced a dull headache every Saturday morning. Searching for the cause, it dawned on him that he drank several cups of coffee each day during the work week. On Saturday, however, when he was without his ordinary supply, he began to go through withdrawal, thus the low-grade pain in his head. His solution was simple: brew a pot of coffee on the weekend and put the caffeine back into his system. His craving was satisfied by a few more cups of coffee, but his physical need for caffeine remained. Similarly, the solution to the alcoholic's hangover, or withdrawal, is to start drinking again. But this only serves to reinforce the craving for alcohol.

Second, we experience loss of *control*. My friend needed his caffeine. The chemical changes in his system were beginning to control him. His answer was to consume more and more coffee in order to end withdrawal symptoms and feel "up." At that point he was out of control. Similarly, drug addicts on the street need to know where their dealer is and when he or she can be reached, so they can know where their supply or "stash" is. With this knowledge they feel in control.

The fear of losing control (which, ironically, has already happened) makes us incredibly controlling. For example, if we are in an addictive relationship, we need to know the whereabouts of the person to whom we are attached. We are jealous of any intrusion into our intimacy by someone from the outside. Fearful of losing the relationship, we hold on ever more tightly. In the words of many popular books, we become people who "love too much."

Third, along with our craving and loss of control, we engage in *continual use*. As we build a tolerance for the object of our addiction, we need more and more intake in order to achieve the same high. Our addictive disease is progressive and leads to obsessions. Believing we can control our addiction, we are, little by little, compulsively controlled by it.[9]

The three Cs were all apparent in my own life. In my case, I *craved* crisis. In the 1960s I used the needs of people in trouble to get my high when I tried to meet those needs. I lived off of the ensuing adrenaline rush. I continually set myself up to be late for appointments just so I could experience an extra rush. I refused to take vacations because I had convinced myself that I was indispensable; my craving would not be satisfied by sitting on some beach. (In fact, if I sat still long enough, my emptiness might be revealed. I might get in touch with emotions that I wanted to repress.) Finally, I craved the success of my ministry and the increasing public recognition that it received.

I also experienced an escalating loss of *control*. I became compulsive. I had to be at every meeting; I had to be directly involved with every conflict and every crisis. I tried to be in control because I felt everything was getting out of control and taking me with it. I thought I had to be on the job day and night, yet my efficiency collapsed. Phone calls and letters went unanswered. I avoided them, in part, because I feared saying no to any request. My personal life became largely nonexistent. And I justified all of this by claiming that I was "serving the Lord," to the max.

No one ever challenged my addictive behavior. In fact, I was applauded for my dedication and success. Based on my unending need for approval, I responded by working all the harder so that I could get more strokes.

This lead me to the third C of addiction, *continual use*. Clearly, as I abused this lifestyle, I built a tolerance for many things that had been challenging at the outset. Now I needed bigger adrenaline fixes. Since I craved more excitement and more of a rush, I became willing to leave the fix the church provided to search for greater fixes. I found some by leading 1960s-style public marches for Jesus down Hollywood Boulevard with big media exposure. It was a rush meeting important people of the era such as Hal Lindsay, Chuck Smith, and Billy Graham. Other fixes could be found by traveling and speaking at large conferences about my successes in Hollywood. Endless airplane tickets made me feel important. *Christianity Today* called me the theologian of the Jesus Movement. After that I found more important fixes by writing books, making a movie about my ministry and getting my own television show. The possibilities seemed endless and well justified.

Through our craving and constant use of various substances and processes, we try to fill what John Bradshaw calls the lonely, empty "hole in the soul." Because of our need to alter our moods, we are set up for addictions to substances such as drugs, alcohol, sugar, caffeine, nicotine, and food. We become controlled by processes, such as sex, work, gambling, television, religion, money, and fear. Some of us experience a more insidious and less recognizable form of addiction to codependent relationships in which we enmesh our lives with another person until we are left with little or no identity of our own.

Most romantic songs lament, "I can't live without you." This, of course, is a lie. It would be more relevant to sing such lyrics to a glass of water. Nevertheless, to many of us, the feelings conveyed in mere songs are real. Without self-worth, codependents seek their value by serving other people and, in turn, making those people dependent on them. Behind this self-seeking care giving lies manipulation, anger, and depression. A recent joke defines a codependent as a dying person who sees someone else's life pass before her eyes. This humorous truth exposes the ultimate emptiness and despair of codependency.

I observed the pain of codependency in a woman who became very dear to me. She was the wife of a busy lawyer and the mother of seven children. Both she and her husband were alcoholics. Most of the children followed suit, becoming drug addicts or alcoholics. She filled her life with monitoring her brood, and she kept most of them dependent and living at home well into their late twenties. She continually served them, doing their laundry and fixing spectacular meals. She rescued them from the consequences of their addictions by paying their bills and speeding tickets and even hiring high-priced lawyers when their abuse got them into trouble. Through her care giving, however, she constantly manipulated them through behaviors such as making them feel guilty if they ate out.

She kept her deep faith, but wondered why her children, fed up with legalism and hypocrisy, fled the church. Her ultimate crisis came when she could no longer pretend to control her addicted sons. Suddenly they were gone into treatment centers or halfway houses. It was then she had to face the hole in her soul. She became sickly, lost weight, and even at times wanted to die. She had lived outside herself for so long that when her human props left, she went with them. Her own recovery continues to be a long process.

The Consequences of Addiction

What happens to us when we don't receive treatment for addiction? Anne Wilson Schaef in *When Society Becomes an Addict,* offers the following points. We find ourselves in denial. *Dishonesty* is the primary symptom. Alcoholics may admit that they drink too much on occasion or that they have "a little drinking problem," but that's as far as their admission goes. They may even promise, "I'll quit tomorrow," but tomorrow never comes.

We are incredibly *self-centered.* There is no one more selfish than an addict needing a "fix." To get it, they will lie, cheat, steal, and even kill. In the panic of the craving, all sense of morality and humanity disappears.

There is also growing *dependency* and obsession with the object of addiction. We believe we can't go on living without it. Then there is the need to *control* our source of supply. Since we are basically out of control of our lives, we try to bring everyone and everything else under our control. This need to control others lies at the core of addiction.[10]

As a pastor, I never saw myself as an addict nor the Church as an addictive institution. I was in denial. If confronted, I would have rejected the fact that I was self-centered. After all, didn't I serve and care for people? Wasn't the call of God upon my life? I failed to see how much I was merely meeting my own needs by getting my "fix" from people. I couldn't imagine that I was using them to justify my life, alter my moods, and give myself a feeling of well-being. Although I failed to see my growing dependency on my ministry, I came to a point when I felt like nothing without it. Since my ministry was my life, I ended up obsessively controlling it. But while I thought that I was controlling it, it was really controlling me. It would eventually grind me into the dust.

The effects of our personal addictions don't end with us. What goes on inside of our addictive selves is projected onto the outside world as we remold it to reflect our addictive experience. As a result, all of us live more and more in what Anne Wilson Schaef calls the addictive process or the addictive culture. This creates a circle; we are addicts imprisoned, yet contributing to, an addictive world.

It is devastating for me to admit that the Church, which is called to be a prophetic voice to its surrounding culture, instead largely mirrors it. The Church is fast becoming an addictive institution in its own right. Rather than converting the world, it is being converted by the world.

Like the addict, our addictive culture and its institutions are *self-centered*. The United States, for instance, is the center of the universe to us. Everything revolves around our national interests.

Once God and the Church become fully identified with each other, the Church becomes self-centered as well. Feeling justified by its divine position in the world, it seeks to save its own life and in the process loses it. If you doubt this self-absorption, check the budget of your local congregation. See where the money goes and how your pastor spends his or her time. You will find that the needs of the flock are busily met while those outside the fold are lucky to get some leftovers. After all, the church must fulfill the needs of those who pay the bills or they won't stick around.

Like the addict, our addictive culture is, in reality, out of control. At the same time, it is controlling and feeds on the *illusion of control*. In Alcoholics Anonymous, the first step in recovery is the admission of powerlessness over unmanageable lives. Nevertheless, in this culture, we try to control everything and everybody. Politically, for example, since the Gulf War and the collapse of the Soviet Union, the United States views itself as the policeman of a "new world order." What an illusion! At best, we may be the policeman of the old world disorder that is now being reshaped by the forces of history and the providential hand of God.

Like our culture, the Church is a controlling institution. Ripped from its context, Paul's dictum to the Corinthians that "everything is to be done in a fitting and orderly way" (1 Cor. 14:40) is the Church's thesis statement. Most congregations on Sunday experience this misguided control from the call to worship to the benediction. Comfort, passivity, and compliance are the intended results.

The addictive culture promotes and rewards the results of *linear and rational thinking.* It doesn't know what to do with right-brain visions, intuition, or creativity. In business, policy manuals mandate that decisions are made "by the book." In the Church, this philosophy is lived out in rigid ecclesiastical order within committees filled with endless reports and study papers.

Underlying such a need to control everything, Schaef says, is the fear of losing control, which creates panic.

Paradoxically, the addictive culture also encourages *confusion.* Keeping people in the dark is another way of maintaining control. Alcoholics on a binge may throw everyone else off, but they know exactly what they want and how to get it. They are sure to get the next drink through intimidation or violence. As the Church mirrors the addictive culture, it creates a confusing theological smoke screen of double-talk and ambiguity. This allows its leaders, who pride themselves in pluralism or relativism, to slide over substantial issues and maintain control.

The addictive culture uses *secrecy* as a form of control. The average person often doesn't know what is going on in a society or institution until it's too late to do anything about certain situations. We use secrecy in considering promotions, executive searches, and faculty appointments. It is also the typical methodology used in calling a pastor to a new church. The process is often well guarded, and the congregation doesn't know who is being considered. It's "against the rules" for such confidences to be broken. Therefore, no one can pray directly about the choice or give honest input about the candidates. Control, held in the hands of a select few members of the nominating committee or a bishop, is the order of the day.

The addictive culture is *crisis oriented*. It creates the illusion of being alive by continually placing the system under stress. We often see this in the alcoholic family. As the alcoholic goes on a binge, the whole family suffers but oddly gains purpose and unity through dealing with the situation. Life now centers around the disease that keeps the family feeling "alive" and together. Likewise, as many historic churches decline in membership and power, their leadership continually places them in false crisis by bringing up issues such as gay ordination, extra- and premarital sex, the environment, and other topical issues of the day. By provoking such crises, these declining churches appear to be alive and well. Their leaders distract their members from the real issues of evangelism, growth, moral character, theological integrity, and social justice by throwing them into spasms of continual controversy.

Dishonesty is also a norm in addictive culture. Society has mastered the art of managing impressions. In the age of MTV and designer labels, image is all important, a matter of public relations. When I was in seminary, I worked for my home church one summer. The Minister of Christian Education planned a day camp for sixty to seventy junior high kids, but only seven registered. Rather than admit his miscalculation, he announced to the congregation that this was a pilot project with limited enrollment. Through his example of managing impressions, he taught me to lie to the church.

The addictive culture is *perfectionistic.* The prevailing motto is "all or nothing." It is rigid, judgmental, and critical. Through perfectionism, society either keeps us striving for the impossible, or it cuts our nerve of action, which throws us into despair.

Thus, perfectionism can breed arrogance, depression, or a sense of failure. We then mask these deep-rooted feelings by denial or through mood-altering activities and relationships. Perfectionism is a hallmark of the addictive church. Whether liberal or evangelical, Catholic or Protestant, most Christians labor under a great burden of legalism. The special behavioral standard set for us by a particular church may be social involvement, personal morality, or sacramental duty. Whatever the requirement, we are expected to conform and are judged accordingly.

Perfectionism suffocates honesty. This dishonesty starts with pastors: They are always supposed to smile, make time for us, and have the right answer. They are to be, as one friend described, "preacher perfect." If ministers disclose personal struggles, they must always be couched in the past tense. After all, congregations must know how pastors triumphed over their crises so they themselves can do the same. Of course, this scenario also helps maintain the Church's illusions of pastoral perfection. Pastor's families are also expected to be perfect. This is the crushing burden that they carry. No wonder so many preachers' kids are rebellious, sexually promiscuous, unbelieving, and flipped out on drugs. Many Christians easily forget that if they could become perfect on their own, there would be no need for the saving power of Jesus.

The addictive culture is also *selective*. It forgets or filters out everything that doesn't fit into its system. For example, the present secularization of mainline churches, with their commitment to theological relativism, has progressed by the denial of their evangelical roots. For many of these churches, their beginnings go back to the Great Awakening prior to the Revolutionary War. They block out the memory of the power of the Holy Spirit working through the revivals of John Wesley, George Whitfield, and Jonathan Edwards, as well as Charles Finney and Dwight L. Moody's later ministries. This forgetfulness helps these churches accommodate their belief in the supremacy of reason and the scientific worldview. This view conveniently locks God's active presence out of the created universe and the Church as well. Rather than admitting their disconnection from their heritage, they give the greatness of their founders faint praise while going about the business of assimilating into the surrounding addictive culture.

The addictive culture creates *dependent relationships*. The system is obsessed with controlling people by keeping them fearful while simultaneously offering them a false security if they submit to it. The vehicles for this intimidation are implied threats of job loss, imprisonment in a pension plan, or the promise of better things to come, which never materialize. In our Churches, we often see this dependency in operation. Vast numbers of people docilely submit to the established hierarchy, jettisoning their minds and their moral responsibility at the sanctuary doors.

Like the addict, the addictive culture hordes its "stash" or source of supply. Because of this, our culture follows the *scarcity model*. We live in fear of never having enough. I have seen this operate in a church, especially around budget time. Creative change is often squelched by the claim, "We just don't have the money." Pledge cards are handed out as a means of guaranteeing the income for the next year. This tactic gives us the illusion of control when we really have none. Who knows what the economy will bring, what big givers will move away, who will die, or who will become disenchanted with what the church is doing? The continual harassment of people in the pews for money is motivated by fear, reflecting the need to guarantee the church's source of supply.

The addictive culture lives negatively and defensively by *denying real feelings*. As in an abusive family, true emotions in many churches are shut down. Negative feelings are especially "bad." Remember hearing, "If you can't say something nice, you better not say anything at all"? One of the severest criticisms leveled against pentecostalism and the Charismatic Movement is that of emotionalism, as if feelings are to be feared rather than welcomed. The denial of feelings leaves us as incomplete people who depend only on reason, disengaged from the rest of reality. At this point, rationalism becomes the test of reality itself.

The addictive culture fosters *"frozen feelings."* In the business environment, emotion is feared as a sign of instability or immaturity rather than as wholeness and integration. Our inner child is controlled by this emotional shutdown. Reason reigns instead, which guarantees that the underlying panic over losing control is never addressed. Likewise, in many churches emotional display is throttled. We direct attention instead to what goes on outside of the self. Architectural aesthetics, liturgy, and music often substitute for spontaneity, genuine feeling, and a fresh encounter with the Holy Spirit.

Finally, the addictive culture produces *ethical deterioration;* the system will do anything to perpetuate itself. Church leaders make the ends justify the means. Standards become relative and everything is contextual. There are no absolute morals such as truth and honesty, which are easily slain on the altar of self-preservation and assimilation into the surrounding environment. It is clear that the Church participates in this ethical deterioration. Moral relativism, hidden under a cloak of loving and accepting everybody, replaces character, making holiness a dead issue.

As Anne Wilson Schaef notes, all of the above characteristics of the "addictive process" or the addictive culture, are born out of fear. Like viruses, they are multiplying with lethal power in the body of the Church. Since we are psychologically, physically, and spiritually preconditioned for addictions, we have all accommodated ourselves to the addictive society. These addictions prosper across denominational and theological lines. However shattering it may be to admit this, our denial must be broken through if healing is to begin. But what is at the root of all of this? Where does the "hole in the soul" originate? The Bible reveals the source of all our addictions and compulsions.

Chapter 2

Getting to the Root
of Our Addictions

.   .   .

Why do people come to Christ but not get better? Why are so many Christians caught in compulsive sickness and sin? I believe the answer to these questions lies in the Church's shallow response to our addictive selves. Most gospel tracts tell us that God loves us and has a wonderful plan for our lives. They go on to reveal that we have missed this plan because of the sin that separates us from God. Jesus is then presented as the bridge to a holy God. If we accept His death for us, God will forgive our sins and give us eternal life. However, the only thing these tracts seem to say to us after we become Christians is, "Good luck."

Such evangelism centers on our personal responsibility. It doesn't consider the contributions that heredity and environment, or nature and nurture, have made to the human condition. The traditional, evangelical message sees the individual in isolation. Salvation is my issue for which I alone am responsible. I am guilty of separating myself from God. I have to decide to repent and accept Jesus as my personal Savior. The stress is upon what each of us must do, not in what God can and will do in our lives through Jesus. This perpetuates the illusion that I as an individual am still in control.

This addictive thinking masks the Christian's most secret sin, that of not giving everything to Jesus and submitting to him as Lord. This self-centeredness also makes people miss the radical nature of evil and grace. In the spiritual world, like the physical world, a superficial diagnosis leads to a partial cure. If we think that we have a skin infection rather than cancer, we will settle for salve rather than surgery. The Church has settled for the salves of personal will-power to explain and cure the deep problems of humanity. The Church is in denial.

The biblical diagnosis of the human condition is much more comprehensive and profound. Consider Ephesians 2:1–3:

> And you were dead in your trespasses and sins, in which you formerly walked according to the course of this world, according to the prince of the power of the air, of the spirit that is now working in the sons of disobedience. Among them we too all formerly lived in the lusts of our flesh, indulging the desires of the flesh and of the mind, and were by nature children of wrath, even as the rest.

In these verses, Paul gives a fivefold diagnosis of our condition. First, we are spiritually dead in trespass and sins. Consequently, we follow the course of this fallen world. This leaves us open to domination by the devil or "the prince of the power of the air." As a result, we indulge the desires of the flesh and mind. Finally, we are under the wrath of God because, in the words of Karl Barth, God says no to the above state of affairs. Since our present condition is not within the original intention of Creation, we stand under God's judgment.

We all suffer from *generational sin*. From birth there is a hole in our soul, making our lives unmanageable. We arrive on this planet spiritually severed from God. In the words of Bob Dylan,

> I was blinded by the devil,
> Born already ruined,
> Stone-cold dead,
> As I stepped out of the womb.[1]

From Adam and Eve to the present, we have inherited a chain of sin. Since generational sin and its resulting sicknesses become progressively worse, we can consider ourselves the victims of accumulated abuse. Our family tree is dysfunctional. As Paul says in Romans 5:20, "sin abounds." Alcoholic parents beget alcoholic children. The abused become abusers. The cycle goes on and on throughout the human bloodline.

Apart from dysfunctional families, we are caught in a more generalized *environmental sin*. We conform to the "course of the world." Although blessed by God's providential care, we live in a culture that has separated itself from him. Only this severed tie can explain the enormity of the evil that we face today: the rampant spread of AIDS; the renewed danger of malaria from the greenhouse effect; the continual depletion of the ozone layer producing a rising threat of cancer; the destruction of tropical rain forests; the abortive slaughter of innocents; the glut of drugs and the accompanying gang violence, oppressive poverty, and starvation. The list goes on and on.

We are controlled by dark spiritual forces, which are demonic hoards, ruled by the "prince of the power of the air." The devil is like a stealth bomber who slips undetected through our natural defenses in order to destroy us. We live in the illusion of our own control. In reality, we're out of control, or more to the point, under alien control. Dysfunctional families have only contributed to this spiritual oppression. Our emotional shutdown and addictive tendencies may be inherited from our family tree, but they have been reinforced by the continuing dysfunctional family environment and spiritually oppressed world.

Finally, we contribute to the sum total of evil by our *personal sin*. At some point, we choose to live within the boundaries of the lusts of our flesh and our weakened human nature. We are not only caught in sin, we like our sinful condition. In Romans 1:32, Paul says,

> . . . although they know the ordinance of God, that those
> who practice such things ("unrighteousness, wickedness,

greed," and the like) are worthy of death, they not only do the same, but also give hearty approval to those who practice them.

Our hearty approval is what we add to the generational and environmental sin into which we are born. We cannot shirk from our resulting moral responsibility.

Now, in light of the legacy that has been spelled out in Ephesians 2:1–3, we must ask ourselves, "What is our core problem? What is the basis for this severe diagnosis?" The answer lies in the beginning. . . .

The first chapter of Genesis reveals that humans were made in the image of God, male and female, and given dominion over this planet. This means that we have been made for a relationship with God. We have also been given rule of this world.

The second chapter of Genesis reveals that our human loneliness is meant to be solved in the permanent, heterosexual, and monogamous context of marriage. The final verse of Genesis 2 shows the ideal state of humanity: In the Garden of Eden, Adam and Eve were "naked and were not ashamed." That is, they were absolutely vulnerable, free, and transparent. Nothing separated them from God or from each other.

In Genesis 3, however, the primeval couple become naked and ashamed. After the Fall, which was triggered by the outside influence of Satan, they sew aprons together to cover their nakedness. With recognition of their nakedness, the shame-based cover-up begins. Hiding from each other and hiding from God, the human race became a permanent factory of apron makers.

Adam and Eve sinned by falling for the presumption that they could run their own lives or "be like God." Their sin was pride, which told them they could live an autonomous existence and be in control of everything. Pride always separates people from God. As Adam and Eve abandoned God, they were, in turn, abandoned by God. It was out of this original abandonment that the shame base for the rest of humanity was established. The experience of abandonment means that the person who is abandoned is left with the feeling of valuelessness. Rejection is a death experience. Yet, while God's abandonment of us in judgment is always relative (God clothed Adam and Eve even as they were expelled from Eden), it feels absolute to us. Our shame base lies at the root of our addictions. But what is shame?

Gershin Kaufmann writes,

> [Shame] is the most poignant experience of the self by the self whether felt in humiliation or cowardice or in a sense of failure to cope successfully with challenge. Shame is a wound felt on the inside, dividing us both from ourselves and from one another.[2]

Commenting on this definition, John Bradshaw distinguishes between healthy shame, which defines our creaturely limits, and toxic shame, which kills us. He writes that toxic shame

> is the source of most of the disturbing inner states which deny full human life. Depression, alienation, self-doubt, isolating loneliness, paranoid and schizoid phenomena, compulsive disorders, splitting of the self, perfectionism, a deep sense of inferiority, inadequacy or failure, the so-called borderline conditions, and disorders of narcissism all result from shame. Shame is a kind of soul murder. Once shame is internalized, it is characterized by a kind of psychic numbness which becomes the foundation for a kind of death in life. Forged in the matrix of our source [family] relationships, shame conditions every other relationship in our lives. Shame is total non-acceptance.
>
> Shame is a being wound—in other words, it has to do with who we are at the deepest level—and differs greatly from the feeling of guilt. Guilt says I've done something wrong; shame says there is something wrong with me. Guilt

says I've made a mistake. Shame says I am a mistake. Guilt says what I did was not good; shame says I *am* no good.[3]

This shame is reinforced down through the generations. When we hear pronouncements from our parents such as "I'm ashamed of *you*," the meaning is not "I'm ashamed of what *you've done*," but "I'm ashamed of who *you are*." Many of us have heard, "You ought to be ashamed of yourself." This exhortation to shame focuses not upon our actions, but upon our being. All of this thrusts the consequences of the Fall deep into us. We become ashamed of shame.

Our abandonment of God causes his abandonment of us. God's love is a holy love that doesn't tolerate sin. Because God respects our being, made in his image, he honors our decision to live without him. (He will not drag us kicking and screaming into heaven.) His inevitable withdrawal creates a deep sense of shame in us. This internal "being wound" is the source of the hole in the soul, that inner existential dread and madness. In despair, we come to believe that at the core of ourselves, is nothing; we are a flash of consciousness in an eternity of unconscious nonbeing.

Our response to this realization is shame. Our response to shame is to try to cover up, for fear of exposure. We fear facing the results of abandonment: depression, aching loneliness, and the loss of our true self. In place of God's image in us, we create the false self, a Hollywood movie set behind which we hide. This screen is made from our own fears and fantasies. The scripts are written by other people. If we are honest, it often seems that we are acting in someone else's movie. We have become people pleasers, trapped by performing in order to gain acceptance.

Our cover-up makes us pass the buck. After the Fall, when God looked for Adam and Eve, he asked them how they discovered their nakedness. Blame started immediately. Adam replied, "The woman . . ." Next, Eve looked for her out and claimed,

"The serpent . . ." The beginning of the dysfunctional family was at work with its addictive, codependent behavior centered in blaming and avoiding responsibility.

A New Testament Update

As we turn to the New Testament, Paul describes this shame-based, false self as a life lived "in the flesh." When we are in the flesh, we carry the illusion of our own autonomy; we rely on ourselves rather than on God; we're propelled by narcissism and pride rather than humility; and we think that we're in control.

The classic expression of the false self, or life in the flesh, is found in Romans 7:14. Here the apostle describes himself as "of the flesh, sold into bondage to sin." Sin is not a mere moral failure. It is a power that holds Paul captive. It is an addiction that he can't lick alone. Later, in verse 18, he confesses, "For I know that nothing good dwells in me, that is, my flesh." This admission contains an important qualification. The "me" of which he speaks is his flesh. His flesh is his false self and is in opposition to his essential, true being created by God.

To be in the flesh, then, is to be under the power of sin and to define ourselves by our addictions. Gerald May says that we even become addicted to our "self-representational system."[4] This system is the way we view ourselves in our various roles as father, mother, husband, wife, and so on. As we become attached to these self-images, they begin to control us.

To live in the flesh, therefore, is to live our lives in addiction. We can't escape it. This is our fallen human condition. Our shame-based lives are now represented by our false selves, which we use to try to fill the holes in our souls.

What should we do with the false self? According to the Bible, there is only one possibility: The false self must die.

Chapter 3

Grace, Grace, Grace

.   .   .

In order for our false selves to die with Jesus, we must break
through denial, detach ourselves from the objects of addiction, go through the pain of withdrawal, acknowledge anger
over loss of these objects, and grieve until the Holy Spirit
comes and heals us. As we die to our false selves, the fear that
lies behind them will be exposed. After that fear is acknowledged, Jesus will come and comfort us, healing the shame that
lies at the base of our lives. It is at this moment that the generational chain of sin can be broken. We are incorporated by God's
Spirit into the true Church and can now be released from our
captivity to the environment of sin in this fallen world. Jesus is
complete help for our all-encompassing needs. Through him
our deep sickness receives a cure that is deeper still. And all
this healing comes to us by grace alone. Why is this so hard to
believe?

Evangelical churches preach a gospel of justification by
faith, but often live a gospel of justification by works. As a
result, they are incredibly religious. They tell people that God
loves them unconditionally, yet at the same time, pile conditions on them before including them in their fellowship. The
status symbols of acceptance can be anything from the mode
of baptism an individual chooses to which Bible translation
someone carries. The hidden agenda is what people must do

for God rather than what God wants to do for people. This blurring of unconditional and conditional love makes us crazy. As my friend Rich Buhler notes in *Love: No Strings Attached,* this craziness is perpetuated in families where approval has been confused with love.[1] As a result, people spend their lives looking for approval when what they really need is love. To say that we need to be loved unconditionally is not sentimental. I don't need to approve of everything others say and do, but if I love them, and they really know it, we will have a secure basis for our relationships and be able to deal with our differences honestly.

By living out the gospel of justification by works, the church merely apes our larger culture. Many children have been subjected to "I love you, *but* . . ." "I love you, *but* clean up your room . . ." "I love you, *but* get good grades . . ." "I love you, *but* go to college . . ." "I love you, *but* go into daddy's business . . ." "I love you, *but* marry a blonde" (they have more fun)." Once I heard one mother thoughtlessly say to her daughter, "If you will do this for me, I'll love you for life." Teachers, coaches, pastors, bosses, and countless friends have used conditionals to prod us and keep us in line. Such experiences leave us with an underlying question, "If I fail to perform or measure up, will you still love me?" The gnawing fear deep down in our souls is that if we don't measure up, we will be rejected. Because of this, we are unable to love ourselves or love others fully and freely.

Conditional love is an absolute contradiction to the good news of the gospel. Jesus showed us the relationship he had with his heavenly Father who never says, "I love you, *but* . . ." As the perfectly loved Son of God, Jesus exhibited a love for his enemies, praying from the cross for their forgiveness. Through Jesus' example, we can believe that God loves us no matter what. Because of our relationship with God we will be motivated to do certain things, but his love for us never depends on

our doing them (or on doing them the way the Church expects
them to be done).

Tragically, when new Christians come to the Church, they
quickly learn the prevailing code of conduct in order to feel
welcome. Failing to find love and acceptance, they fight instead
for approval. What a certain congregation deems as cultural
sins must quickly leave the lives of new believers. "Chris-
tianeez" punctuates ordinary speech. Evangelicals are careful
to use "Praise the Lord" or "God told me . . ." while liberals
insert "pluralism," "dialogue," and "empowerment" in the right
spot. The false self, resulting cover-up, and life in the flesh continue as all of us become religious performers. Tragically this
kind of life keeps Christians emotionally and spiritually sick.
Ironically, Jesus came to do away with such religious performances. It was this system that ultimately killed him, and it will
kill us.

A Fresh Look at Jesus' Ministry

When Jesus launched his public ministry, three things happened. First, God's kingdom was manifested through him to
prostitutes and thieves as well as law-abiding types. Second,
hurting, lonely people "undressed" before the good physician,
revealing their deepest pain and receiving His healing touch
(and they didn't do anything to deserve it). Finally, Jesus' ministry immediately set off a negative reaction. What Jesus said and
did threatened the whole religious establishment. It undercut
the thesis of the law: performance for acceptance. If you were
good, God would reward you. (And still, today, those of us who
hold religious power get to define "good.") In Jesus' presence,
false selves were exposed so religion could no longer control
people.

This challenge to the establishment is portrayed in the Gospel of Mark. No sooner did Jesus launch his messianic ministry by gathering disciples, casting out demons, and healing

people, than the religious leaders began to oppose him. In the second chapter of Mark, Jesus did four instructive things: challenged the accepted basis of salvation; changed the meaning of community; negated common piety; undercut public morality. No wonder the Pharisees had murderous thoughts toward him and immediately began to plot his death.

First, Jesus challenged the accepted basis of salvation when he forgave a man's sins and commanded him to take up his bed and walk. Forgiveness became, in that instant, not only a theological idea but an actual event. As Jesus was speaking his word of grace, the scribes watched and thought: "Why does this man speak that way? He is blaspheming; who can forgive sins but God alone?" (Mark 2:7).

Up until then, forgiveness had been centered in the temple, the priesthood, and the sacrificial system. The holy God could only be approached through an elaborate blood ritual. This entire intricate system, however, was simply to prepare Israel for the final sin sacrifice that, according to the Prophet Isaiah, would be made by the Suffering Servant of the Lord. (See Isaiah 53.) He would come, bearing God's forgiveness in his own person and offering his own blood for humanity. He would be "the Lamb of God who takes away the sin of the world" (John 1:29). This Lamb was Jesus.

It became right and proper for Jesus to exercise God's forgiveness with authority on earth. In so doing, he fulfilled the whole religious system in himself. In other words, the priests and their sacrifices were superseded by him. They lost their control over Israel's access to God. Like the medieval monks after Luther's Reformation, they could no longer corrupt and market forgiveness. Sheer grace threw them out of a job. Jesus wasn't controlled by them when he stood before the paralytic and pronounced, "My son, your sins are forgiven" (Mark 2:5). If this was true, who would buy the sacrificial animals? Who would pay for the maintenance of the temple? Who would feed the priests? Who would frequent the merchants in Jerusalem, who profited by pilgrim visits? The system of forgiveness had been replaced by the person of Jesus and his once-and-for-all sacrifice for sins. It wasn't surprising that there was an immediate reaction against the power of God to forgive and restore the frozen boy dropped at Jesus' feet. Either this was blasphemy, or God himself had stepped forward. Religion was out of business.

Jesus not only overturned the whole system of forgiveness by placing the basis of salvation in himself, he also undercut the whole religious understanding of community. For Jews at that time, God was holy. Since they were to be a holy people (and this is defined by legalistic, perfectionistic thinking), then they had to be separate. They defended their holiness by carefully excluding pagans and sinners from their midst. (Church addicts in their self-centeredness do the same.) After all, "a man is known by the company he keeps." Religious, holy people needed to be with other religious, holy people. Through obedience and moral purity, they would be a witness of God's laws. This was their special calling in life. They were to live aloof from this sinful, fallen, horrid, debauched world. Their whole understanding of community was *exclusive*.

Then Jesus came. He didn't see God's community as exclusive but as *inclusive*. His relationships weren't based on fear. He didn't have the fear of being contaminated or exposed, the fear of being seen with the wrong people and of losing control of his reputation. So how did he live his life? He ate with taxgatherers and sinners. Today he stands with pimps, prostitutes, bikers, drug addicts, mafia hitmen, corrupt politicians, shysters, loan sharks, pushers, illegal aliens, transvestites, drag queens, and inside traders. These are the people that Jesus now invites to dinner. He actually enjoys hanging out with these folks.

Doesn't this make you mad? Doesn't this offend you? It certainly had that effect on the religious leaders of Jesus' day. The people he was seen with were the people that we wouldn't want in our neighborhoods. They were the people we would never want our daughters to date. Today, standing at our church doors on Sunday, we politely suggest to similar people that they find another fellowship more suited to their place in life. We believe this suggestion is really in their best interest; they would be much happier with their own kind (we're certainly not *their* kind).

Mark 2:16 tells us, "And when the scribes of the Pharisees saw that He [Jesus] was eating with the sinners and tax-gatherers, they began saying to His disciples, 'Why is He eating and drinking with tax-gatherers and sinners?'" The religious reaction against Jesus deepened.

God's heart was open to all. God's love was revealed to be inclusive rather than exclusive. There was now no them and us—our kind and their kind. Consider Jesus' reply to the religious people of his day, "It is not those who are healthy who need a physician, but those who are sick; I did not come to call the righteous, but sinners" (Mark 2:17). For us this means that we as addicts are now welcome into God's kingdom.

Third, after Jesus centered forgiveness in himself and welcomed all to his table, he began to offend the prevailing religious sensitivities concerning common piety. He refused to require his disciples to fast. Apparently he did not glory in the mortification of the flesh. He didn't advocate not eating as a necessary sign of godly repentance and sorrow. His irreligious attitude led the Pharisees to ask Jesus, "Why do John's disciples and the disciples of the Pharisees fast, but your disciples do not fast?" (Mark 2:18).

Jesus' answer was bold. He was having a party with his men. In Mark 2:19 he compared his time with them to a wedding feast: "While the bridegroom is with them, the attendants of the bridegroom do not fast, do they? So long as they have the bridegroom with them, they cannot fast." It wasn't a time for religious, pious acts; it was a time for gladness. It was a time of salvation, victory, freedom, and release. It was a time to enjoy the presence of the Messiah. It was party time! The whole legalistic structure of external disciplines and physical mortification was exploded: It was no longer the law, but the gospel; it was no longer religion, but relationship; it was no longer Moses, but an unmitigatedly joyful life with Jesus. The solemnity of long-faced religious processions was over. It was time to become like little children in order to enter the kingdom. It was time to dance and sing with Jesus.

Finally, after dealing with forgiveness, fellowship, and piety, Jesus overturned public morality by allowing his disciples to break the law. Hungry, they picked heads of grain on the Sabbath, which provoked a religious reaction, "And the Pharisees were saying to him, 'See here, why are they doing what is not lawful on the Sabbath?'" (Mark 2:24). Jesus answered that if the Sabbath was made for humanity, then why would God want us to go hungry on this special day of worship and celebration? Besides, it was Jesus, not the religious legalists, who now had authority concerning the Sabbath: "Consequently, the Son of Man is Lord even of the Sabbath" (Mark 2:28).

If we took the words and spirit of Jesus seriously today, what would happen to our "blue laws"? What would happen to church attendance? How could the religious hierarchy continue to control people's behavior? What would become of public morality? Life is spontaneous and free with Jesus. While people exploit the law in order to control others, grace seemingly puts us out of control, or better yet, places us under God's control. This grace releases the power of the Spirit within us to be the whole people that we were created to be.

Jesus himself broke the Sabbath law by healing a man's withered hand in the synagogue. During that scene the Pharisees were watching to see if he really would go through with it. Wise counsel would have told Jesus to wait a few hours so as not to provoke them. After all, this man had had his infirmity for a long time. He could hold on a bit longer. But no, Jesus wasn't interested in wise counsel; he was interested in loving this man. It was his mission to overturn a religion that would withhold healing for the sake of a few more pious hours. This moment was the last straw for religion. Not only did Jesus center forgiveness in himself, explode the boundaries of community, and party rather than fast, but he also attacked the whole understanding of public life. The nation of Israel was to reflect God's actions in its actions. Since Yahweh rested on the Sabbath, they were to rest on the Sabbath. But with Jesus, the whole structure collapsed. Mercy triumphed over judgment. Matters of the heart replaced habit. Mourning turned into joy. In effect, religion was losing control. Mark 3:6 says, "And the Pharisees went out and immediately began taking counsel with the Herodians against Him, as to how they might destroy Him."

It's important for us today to see how we use religion to cover up the fear and shame that binds us. It's crucial that we understand how religion uses the law to separate us from our true selves and from each other, creating false selves instead. Religion is life in the flesh. It's life centered on our selves and our own self-justification before God and before each other. Religion can, and often does, become a vehicle for our addictive selves. We use religious practices, aesthetics, and morality to fill the hole in the soul. Religion becomes a means of both manipulating and gaining position with God. As we become religious, we say to God, "Look at my piety, my faith, and my obedience. This ought to impress you. (It impresses me and my friends well enough!) This ought to give me standing with you. You are lucky to have me on your team."

We bargain, manipulate, and try to impress God and each other in order to mask our shame base and overcome the abandonment that sin has left. None of these tricks work. There is no permanent deliverance from addiction through morality or discipline. Paul cries out, "Who will deliver me from the body of this death?" This is the right question. We, however, ask, "*What* will deliver me?" If we can't drink alcohol, then at least we can smoke and drink coffee! If nicotine and caffeine don't help, there are always rehabilitation programs, self-help manuals, therapy groups, new medications, and, of course, religion. All of these fillers may offer some help at a given moment, but they don't address bottom line issues. There is no "what" that will deliver us from addiction. It will merely become the next object of our attachment—the next vehicle for our addictive selves. The deepest need of our lives is not to quit drinking. The deepest need of our lives is to know God. Indeed, only after we have answered the question *"Who will deliver me?"* will we be ready for all the healthy support and spiritual disciplines that others can give us.

The Great Restoration

Jesus is the "who." He delivers us. He overturns the religion of this addictive, dysfunctional world, bringing the Almighty to us as our loving God and restoring our relationship with Him. Jesus bridges the gulf. Our abandonment of God in the garden of Eden has been overcome by undying and triumphant love. God's passionate affirmation is spoken to us through Jesus. Rather than waiting for us to come, God takes the initiative and comes to us.

Life with Jesus is both crisis and process. He is our perfection, and we are becoming like him. For addicts, this process includes giving up control daily, detaching ourselves from compulsions, and accepting God's sovereign, holy love. When will it all end? The process will only be completed when we are face to face with the "who" who delivers us. Jesus is grace, grace, grace.

Chapter 4

At Home with the Father

. . .

In John 14:8 Jesus was asked, "Show us the Father and we shall be satisfied." He answered by claiming, "He who has seen me has seen the Father. . . ." What did Jesus mean when he called God "Father"? How does this revelation relate to our need to fill the hole in the soul?

The revelation of God as Father was one of the unique aspects of Jesus' self-consciousness and ministry.[1] Unlike the Old Testament writers who thought of God as a king or judge, Jesus called God "Abba." This Hebrew family word is translated as "Papa" or "Daddy." J. B. Phillips renders it as "Father, dear Father."[2] Through this, Jesus, as the Son of God, revealed a special relationship with the one, true, holy God with whom he had been intimate from all eternity. This is why Jesus said, "All things have been handed over to me by my Father; and no one knows the Father, except the Son, and anyone to whom the Son wills to reveal Him" (Matt. 11:27).

It is this concept of God as "Abba" that Jesus continues to bring us today. He wants us to experience the same parent/child relationship that he himself enjoys. Jesus adopts us into the heavenly family after we are reborn from above. Only this experience will heal our "being wound." This alone will fill the hole in the soul.

It is because of this heavenly adoption that Jesus taught his disciples to pray as he prayed, "Our Father who art in heaven . . ." (Matt. 6:9, KJV). Likewise, Paul said in Galatians 4:6 that

God sends the Spirit of his Son into hearts—the Spirit that cries, "Abba! Father!" As children of God we respond to Christ's Spirit in the same way, "For you have not received a spirit of slavery leading to fear again, but you have received [the] . . . [S]pirit of adoption as sons by which we cry out, 'Abba! Father!'" (Rom. 8:15). This is the shout of a people set free.

The classic parable of the prodigal son in Luke 15:11–32 makes this heavenly relationship clear. Here the contrast between Jesus and religion is bold and dramatic.

Jesus told the story to a group of religious leaders who were threatened and incensed because of the people he hung out with. He ate with tax-gatherers and sinners. To have a meal with them was his sign of love and hospitality. Rather than condemning these reprobates, he welcomed them to his table, saying, in effect. "I am yours and you are mine." This drove religious people crazy. What kind of a God suspends his holy laws and welcomes such trash into his presence?

This parable is a confrontational narrative that shows religious people like us that God loves unconditionally. God is the Father who overcomes our separation from him by releasing us from our shame and bringing us home to his heart. It's helpful to look at this dramatic story as if it were a play in three acts. Act One shows us the younger son's departure from his father's house. Act Two shows us his return and reunion with his father. Act Three shows us his older brother's reaction and draws the appropriate conclusion. Before the first act beings, let's review the story:

> A certain man had two sons, and the younger of them said to his father, "Father, give me the share of the estate that falls to me." And he divided his wealth between them. And not many days later, the younger son gathered everything together and went on a journey into a distant country, and there he squandered his estate with loose living.

Now when he had spent everything, a severe famine occurred in that country, and he began to be in need. And he went and attached himself to one of the citizens of that country, and he sent him into his fields to feed swine. And he was longing to fill his stomach with the pods that the swine were eating, and no one was giving anything to him.

But when he came to his senses, he said, "How many of my father's hired men have more than enough bread, but I am dying here with hunger! I will get up and go to my father, and will say to him, 'Father, I have sinned against heaven, and in your sight; I am no longer worthy to be called your son; make me as one of your hired men.'" And he got up and came to his Father. . . .

Act One

As the curtain rises, we see a father with his two sons in the living room of the family home. The younger one speaks: "Dad, I can't wait for you to die. Give me my share of the inheritance and I'm out of here." In other words, he wants out of the relationship to the point of holding a deathwish against his dad. It's amazing that this son has the gall to say this to his father. I can't imagine going to my dad with such a request. How would we react if our kids came to us and said, "I want you out of my life. I don't care if you live or die, I want my inheritance now"? This, however, is exactly what we have done to God by rebelling against him and going our own way.

Even more surprising, the father actually grants his son's request. This is incomprehensible, but it is exactly what God has done for us. He lets us go, bankrolling us with his providence and provision while we shake our fist and leave.

The younger son lives in the illusion that he'll find freedom far from his father's house. Well-heeled and with his new false self in place, he thinks, "I am my own person. I am autonomous.

I can now self-actualize myself." Loaded with cash, he departs for a far country. (Today he might go away to college.) As Helmut Thielicke says, his deception is in his denial that all that he has comes from his father's hand.[3]

Once in a far country, as long as the younger son has money he has friends. Unwisely, he exhausts his resources in "loose living." Circumstances now turn against him. A severe famine sets in. Stripped of everything, he's in dire straits. Finally, in desperation, he finds a job feeding pigs—not a great occupation for young Jewish boy. As payment, he can eat at the trough along with the swine.

I imagine him down there, elbowing the porkers out of the way and thinking, "Things could be better." In disgrace and despair, he finally comes to himself. At last, circumstances force him to face reality. His life is out of control. He hits bottom. God's intervention begins by breaking through his denial. His illusion of autonomy is now exposed, and he gets homesick. He remembers how good it really was back at his father's house. Through the crisis, he determines to return home. His rebellion over, he repents.

The younger son, however, is still only capable of understanding his own view of his father. He believes he can't be restored; after all, he has spent his inheritance and dishonored the family name. Dad's honor must be defended. Justice must be done.

Resourceful as ever, he comes up with a plan. Since his father's servants have more than he does, he will go home and say, "Father, I have sinned against heaven and earth and am no longer worthy to be called your son." His admission of guilt will then lead him to make a proposition: "Make me as one of your hired servants." While the younger son knows that he will never be restored to the family, he hopes that there will still be a hint of compassion in his father's heart. If so, at least he can live with the hired help and have a roof over his head and food on the table.

Notice that through this plan, he still maintains control. He doesn't simply cast himself on his father's mercy; he comes home to strike a bargain. This bargaining is his true subtle sin. Like any codependent, he manipulates, regardless of how self-effacing he appears. With plan in hand, he starts his return journey as the curtain drops on Act One.

Let's turn back to the biblical text before the second act begins:

> But while he was still a long way off, his father saw him, and felt compassion for him, and ran and embraced him, and kissed him. And the son said to him, "Father, I have sinned against heaven and in your sight; I am no longer worthy to be called your son." But the father said to his slaves, "Quickly bring out the best robe and put it on him, and put a ring on his hand and sandals on his feet; and bring the fattened calf, kill it, and let us eat and be merry; for this son of mine was dead, and has come to life again; he was lost, and has been found." And they began to be merry.

Act Two

When the curtain rises again, the scene shifts back to the father's house. There we see the father, faithfully scanning the horizon, hoping to catch a glimpse of his renegade son. As the son approaches, I imagine him nervously rehearsing the little speech that he has written on the cuff of his sleeve: "Father, I have sinned against heaven, and in your sight; I am no longer worthy to be called your son; make me as one of your hired men." Head bowed, he comes up the walk.

The father now does the unthinkable. Spotting his son, he rushes out, throws his arms around him, hugs him, and begins to kiss him. The situation at this point appears ludicrous to us. While the father's body language communicates total love and acceptance, the boy doesn't pick up on this. His worldview won't allow for his father's reaction. He is on another track. In his mind, his dad would never act this way. He assumes that he can't be welcomed home and restored to the family. This assumption is faulty, however, because he doesn't really know his father. The son can only think of him as being just and righteous. Similarly, religious people can only think of God as an accountant who keeps an exact ledger of credits and debits. What matters to this holy bookkeeper is performance. They think God approves or disapproves of them based on what they do or don't do, rather than loving them unconditionally for who they are.

While the father bathes his boy in love, the son, unable to compute the hugs and kisses, begins his speech: "Father, I have sinned against heaven, and in your sight; I am no longer worthy to be called your son. . . ." No sooner does he admit his guilt, than the father cuts him off. All the father wants to hear is, "Dad, I've blown it." The son can't initiate his deal. The picture he had of his father is contradicted as his dad graciously intercepts him.

After the embraces, the father gives his son a signet ring and calls for the servants to get him a new suit of clothes. These gestures restore the younger son's status and identity in the family. Next, the servants kill a fattened calf for a welcome home party. Later that evening, I can imagine the younger son walking through the living room surrounded by his celebrating friends, wondering, "Is this really happening to me? I'm home free and there's a party for me." The curtain drops on Act Two.

Let's hear the end of the story from the biblical text before we move on to Act Three:

Now his older son was in the field, and when he came and approached the house, he heard music and dancing. And he summoned one of the servants and began inquiring what these things might be. And he said to him, "Your brother has come, and your father has killed the fattened calf, because he has received him back safe and sound."

But he became angry, and was not willing to go in, and his father came out and began entreating him. But he answered and said to his father, "Look! For so many years I have been serving you, and I have never neglected a command of yours; and yet you have never given me a kid, that I might be merry with my friends, but when this son of yours came, who has devoured your wealth with harlots, you killed that fattened calf for him."

And he said to him, "My child, you have always been with me, and all that is mine is yours. But we had to be merry and rejoice, for this brother of yours was dead and has begun to live, and was lost and has been found."

Act Three

As the curtain rises on the final act, the older brother has been working all day. As he returns, he sees lights and hears music and dancing. He learns from the servant that his younger brother has come home and been fully restored to the family. Even more infuriating, despite all that the older son has done, his father has never killed even a goat so that he can have a party for his friends. Is this justice? Where is the reward for his faithful performance?

Incensed at the news, he defiantly remains outside. Feeling self-justified, like many religious people, he believes in performing in order to be accepted. He is like a faithful church elder. He ushers every Sunday; he sings in the choir; he teaches Sunday school and carries a well-marked Bible; he tithes and shows up at every meeting. He reads religious books (even ones on addiction). He is Mr. Faithful, totally predictable. In other words, he's under the Law. When he hears that his renegade younger brother has been welcomed back into the family,

he rages at such grace. We can see our codependent, workaholic selves in the older son. We're addicted to performance
and gaining God's approval. Fearful that we will never get it,
we become hurt and angry.

Back on stage, the father comes out of the house and begs
his older son to join the party. Resentful, manipulative, never
fulfilled, never satisfied, and filled with "righteous indignation," the older son refuses. He fumes, "How could his father
welcome this rascally younger brother home?" After all, he
rebelled against their dad and spent all of his money on harlots.
(The mention of harlots is new information. Does he know this
or, like many of us, is he making assumptions?) Filled with self-
justification, the older son parades the history of his faithful-
ness before his father: He is the model son; he has never rebelled; he's up at the crack of dawn; he always punches in and
punches out; he has callouses on his hands from working. In
short, he has always tried to please his father, hoping to earn his
approval. The more he tried to fill the hole in his soul by performing, however, the larger the hole became.

Like the older brother, we try to fill our souls with religious
performance, but religion like this never ultimately satisfies. It
wears us down and wears us out, leaving us exhausted.

As the play comes to an end, the father tells his older son
that everything that the father has is his. All the grace the father
extended to the rebellious son is for the righteous son as well.
It was only proper to welcome back the wayward son with
celebration; after all, his return created an opportunity for
grace to pour out from the father's heart. There doesn't need to
be any more justification for joy than grace, simply grace. A son
had been lost and is now found. He had been dead and is now
alive. The son is a living example of being loved for who you
are rather than for what you do.

The younger son masked his rebellion and fear by leaving
home, and in the process, created an autonomous false self. He
thought that when he returned, he would spend his life with

the servants. He would be in a kind of purgatory—around the house but never a part of the household. He never imagined that he would be restored to his position in the family.

His older brother agreed entirely with this perception of reality. He had remained home, masking his anger and fear of rejection by building his performing false self. He was offended that his father would welcome his scalawag younger brother back. His father's behavior seemed unjust and irrational. Ironically, this drama reveals that neither son knew his father. Both thought he was a legalistic bookkeeper demanding performance for his acceptance. Both confused approval for love. Both were prodigal. The father had to crack through both sons' illusions of autonomy and performance, shattering their perceptions of him and of themselves.

It's interesting to note that the father came out of the house twice. Through this simple gesture, he loved each son equally. He had grace not only for the lost son, but also for the "perfect" son. The real difference, then, between the brothers is how each one accepted grace once it was revealed. The younger son was ready and overwhelmed by mercy beyond belief. Since he had nothing more to lose, he had everything to gain by accepting unmerited grace. The prideful older son, however, resisted his father and refused to join the party. In order to defend his own merit and righteousness, he had to retain his own picture of what he thought his father should be. Like so many of us today, he was always addictively around the house, but never joined the party.

Jesus used this dramatic story to reveal the heart of God as that of a loving father. God comes to us in love and wants us to enjoy the party of his free and full grace. This is not a time for fasting; it's a time to sit at his banquet table. The issue is not performance or approval. The issue is massive, boundless, endless love. This is the Father's heart. It's this love that overcomes the feeling of abandonment that all of us inherited from the garden of Eden—a feeling reinforced by each of us going our separate ways. God's love comes with hugs and kisses, destroying our deep shame produced by that sense of separation from himself. Love releases us from our addictive attachments and welcomes us home. This is the good news that Jesus continues to bring to our addictive and codependent selves. There is a party waiting for us in our heavenly Father's heart. His is the joy before the holy angels when one sinner repents. All we have to do is to come to him.

But how can we believe that this story about the father and his two sons is a true reflection of God? I once heard Helmut Thielicke say in a sermon, "We can believe that the story is true because of the third Son, the Son who tells the story." Jesus alone lived in perfect communion with the Father. Jesus alone never experienced abandonment. While all of us are naked and ashamed, he was naked and unashamed, even on the cross.

A Fresh Look at the Crucifixion

In the passion narrative, Jesus was constantly victimized by verbal and physical abuse. Yet he remained unashamed. Three specific instances occurred during Jesus' last hours where others try to make him feel shame. As he goes to the cross, his prophetic gift, kingly rule and saving work were derided.

At his trial, Jesus' prophetic gift was mocked. He was a prophet to the people, bearing the Word of God. His prophecies were both declarative and predictive. He prophesied the destruction of the temple and the fall of Jerusalem. He prophesied Peter's denial and Judas's betrayal. He even predicted the abuse he would receive at the hands of the religious leaders, and they hated him for it. After his trial before the Sanhedrin he was mocked for all of this. They blindfolded him and struck him, demanding, "Prophesy!" (Mark 14:65). He didn't descend to their level. Revelation is not given on abusive demand; so he kept silent.

Following Jesus' trial, his kingly rule was mocked. The heart of his message had been that the kingdom of God was at hand. He proclaimed the kingdom through his words and manifested its power through his works. Thus he was exercising sovereignty over the enemies of God when he cast out demons and healed the sick. Condemned to death by the Roman governor, robed in purple, and crowned with thorns, he was spat upon and struck. Calling him "King of the Jews," the soldiers bowed before him in feigned submission (Mark 15:19). Little did they know that legions of angels were being kept a bay as the soldiers ridiculed the Son of the Almighty God.

Finally, Jesus' saving work was mocked. He had already told people that he had come to seek and save the lost. Going further, he said that he came not to be ministered to but to minister and to give his life as ransom. He had promised his disciples a new covenant through his blood when he celebrated Passover with them. He knew the new covenant was a divine necessity that would be accomplished by his suffering, death, and resurrection in Jerusalem. After he carried his cross through the hooting mob, he was stripped naked and nailed by hands and feet to that cross, which was then thudded into a pothole. He was left to die in bleeding, heaving, blinding, and suffocating agony.

The enraged religious leaders tried to make him feel shame for the very thing that he had come to do. They cried, "Save yourself and come down from the cross! . . . He saved others; he cannot save himself" (Mark 15:30–31, RSV). Their torments had no effect. Jesus maintained his silence through all this humiliation. He was not "ashamed of shame" because, in the darkness as the demons chattered, the Father was with him. He was the true prophet bearing the Word of God. He was the true King, ushering in the kingdom of God. He was the true Savior, sacrificing himself for the world. He had nothing to hide until that awful moment when the sin of the world was laid on his back, thrusting a pain into the Father's heart.

Jesus was naked and unashamed. He still can and does take on our shame for us. On the cross, accepting the penalty for humanity's sins, he freely gave himself over to feeling the abandonment of God's judgment. When we accept Jesus and his free gift of salvation today, it breaks our own shame base. We can reveal our deep inner loneliness and all the twisted perversity of our hearts to him. We can admit the emptiness, the nonbeing at the core of our being. That Jesus knew this emptiness and nonbeing is reflected in his cry, "My God, my God, why hast Thou forsaken me?" (Mark 15:34). At that moment he experienced separation from the Father. Acting as the sin-bearer, he took the punishment and shame of the world on himself. Finally, it was finished.

The word of love became the work of love. Jesus' embrace from the cross was the embrace of the Father, who loves freely and takes us to himself. Through atonement, God didn't change himself. (His grace has been on us from eternity.) He did change the basis of our relationship with him. As sin was paid for, God's justice was upheld and his mercy was released simultaneously. As we experience his forgiving, sacrificial love today, our illusions are shattered. As we experience his resurrected, triumphant presence, life begins. Now, as we are lifted across the threshold to the Father's heart, we hear, "Welcome home!" God has come to fill the holes in our souls—with himself.

The Staggering Implication

My own experience after twenty-seven years of professional ministry leads me to believe that Christians have an incredibly difficult time accepting this simple message of our heavenly Father's unconditional love. Their conscience and religious upbringing rise up against this concept. "What about the holiness of God? What about the Law? Aren't we called to keep it?" The Church reaffirms this response by insisting upon our sacramental duties, moral obedience, faithful attendance, evangelical fervor, social responsibility. While we have clearly proclaimed the message of justification by faith, it has often been muddied by the lifestyle of justification by works. In most congregations, people learn quickly that they will only be accepted if they perform properly.

Peggy, a pastor's daughter, came to me for counseling. She was in much personal pain. As we talked, I asked her what it had been like to grow up in church. She remembered as a small girl that a woman had caught her drawing in a hymnal and scolded, "You shouldn't be doing that. Your father is the pastor!" Later, when she started school, her friends response to her father's vocation was, "Watch it! Her father's a pastor." She withdrew as expectations about her piled up. While she shared these experiences, I began to suspect that Peggy could hardly believe in God's unconditional love for her.

With this in mind, I proposed the following situation, "Peggy, what if you came home on a Friday night dead drunk, opened the front door, staggered in, and vomited? Now suppose Jesus was there in the flesh. What would he do?"

She was silent for a long moment as beads of sweat appeared on her forehead. Her muscles tensed and she began to frown. Finally, she bit out her measured reply, "He—would—be—angry." Then with emphasis, she repeated, "He would be angry!"

After a pause, I asked Peggy if I could tell her what I thought Jesus would do. She agreed. "First," I told her, "he would put you to bed. Then he would clean up your vomit. Finally, when you woke up in the morning, he would put his arms around you and ask, 'Peggy, where does it hurt?'" This is the gospel. This is the only good news for dark souls in the dark world. The lights are on. Welcome home!

Once we've responded to our heavenly Father's love, we're still left with our false selves. To some degree, we continue to live dysfunctional shame-based lives. Our "insides" still seem to be cut off from the presence and power of God. The problem is that while the issue of our own *personal* sin has been resolved, we've never been healed of the many effects of that sin. As a result, they manifest in the construction of our false selves and in our addictive attachments. We've never addressed our *generational* inheritance of sin and the false pedagogy that molded us. Compounding this situation, we continue to live in the *environment* of sin. The addictive society and its institutions that surround us determine, even now, much of the Church.

What can be done about "life in the flesh" and the world system that supports it? What can be done about the autonomous false self, which is revealed either by wild rebellion "in the far country" or by manipulative codependency "around the house"? Unlike modern secular theory, the Bible never proposes that people build self-esteem out of fallen selves or what it calls the "natural man." It never suggests that fallen nature can be exorcised like some raging demon.

Only one possibility for new life is left. The flesh must die. The Christian life begins in death—that is how radical the Gospel really is. Jesus says to his disciples, "If anyone wishes to come after Me, let him deny himself, and take up his cross, and follow Me" (Mark 8:34). (Notice he doesn't say deny your personality but your false self, which we create to cover up the shame inside.) For us to take up the cross doesn't mean merely bearing our little burdens unaided throughout our lives. It's not living with a perpetual rock in our shoes that we can't shake. And it's not paying for individual or generational sins to a bean-counting bill-collecting God.

What many Christians miss is that we not only need to die to our personal sins but also to the generational sin that we've inherited and the environment of sin in which we continue to live. This means that we have to die to the false self and its attachments, created for us by the sins of our parents, our abusive upbringing, and our need to hide our fears, repressed feelings, and shame.

To take up the cross means to bear the instrument of our own death from the judgment hall to Calvary. It means to follow Jesus through his rejection and abandonment and to die with him. Knowing this, Paul witnesses,

> I am crucified with Christ [that is, my attachments have died with Christ] nevertheless, I live [my true self appears], yet not I [not the false self, the independent ego], but Christ lives . . . in me [I'm no longer separated from God but restored]; and the life which I now live in the flesh [in this human reality], I live by faith in the Son of God who loved me, and gave Himself for me." (Gal. 2:20, KJV)

At the point that God intervenes, causing us to hit bottom, we die with Christ. Like Jesus, whose shame was exposed on the cross, our own shame must be acknowledged, exposed, and released. At the cross, we fearfully and painfully lift up everything to the pierced hands of Jesus. As Gerald May notes,

> The loss of attachment is the loss of something very real; it is physical. We still resist this loss as long as we possibly can. When withdrawal does happen, it will hurt. And, after it is over, we will mourn. Only then, when we have completed the grieving over our lost attachment will we breathe the fresh air of freedom with appreciation and gratitude.[4]

Relentlessly, Christ will not let us go until this is complete.

What happens when we begin to understand this comprehensive reality of the gospel and how it applies to our addictions and codependencies? What do we find behind our false selves when they are confronted with the cross and dismantled?

First, we find fear—the fear of exposure, the fear of knowing ourselves and being known, and the fear of giving up our addictions.

At the cross, however, fear must come to light. As it does, its power is broken, for, "perfect love casts out fear" (1 John 4:18). Jesus comes and takes those fearful, small, vulnerable children inside us all, and embraces them in his arms.

Even in the light of Christ's love we may feel a shame that comes from our fallen separation from God: "If you reject me, I must be worthless. If you withdraw your love from me, I must be unlovely. If you leave me, I'll feel unworthy. If you reject me, I'll be ashamed of who I am." Miraculously, it's exactly this fragmented, abused person that Jesus loves and comes to save.

He says, "Let me touch your shame base, your inner-being wound. I am here. I love you. I will never leave you nor forsake you. The abandonment is over. Nothing will take you out of my hand. Nothing will separate you from my love."

After confronting our fears, Jesus confronts the lies with which we've been conditioned. He sees through our disguises and isolation. His truth exposes perfectionism, self-judgments, and the "oughts" and "shoulds" that dominate us. He frees us so we can begin to believe in his love rather than in the performance God's Law demands, our parents' scripts for us, or the expectations of this fallen world.

He also begins to heal anyone that has suffered from violence or abuse. I heard Judith MacNutt tell of a rector who was chronically beaten as a child by schoolyard bullies. As a result, he became a fearful and introverted adult. When Judith prayed for his healing, Jesus gave him a vision. The rector was taken back to that specific schoolyard where he had stood alone against the bullies. They appeared and began walking toward him. As he turned around, he saw Jesus standing behind him. When the bullies got close, Jesus stepped in front of him and said to them, "If you have to hit someone, hit me." With this vision, the rector was healed from a life of fears. This is the same Jesus who takes the abuse for us and sets us free.

As we release our justified anger over the abuse inflicted on us, forgive our enemies and ourselves for our sinful responses, and grieve over childhood loses, Jesus closes the wounds and fills the empty spaces in our souls. By his name, any demonic influence that has used such intrusions to enslave our spirits must flee. By his love he begins to separate us from the objects of our attachments. He stops our chronic psychic bleeding and heals our hearts. And he does all this simply because we're his children. We're children who are finally able to accept his unconditional love, without the conditions of being kind, nice, productive, and well behaved.

Since we've been made in the image of God, we've also been made for a relationship with Jesus. He's the "Second Adam," who through a new spiritual birth brings a whole new humanity into being. Through our relationship with Jesus, the broken image of God that was shattered by the Fall is restored. Jesus' presence in our lives lances our shame base at its core, while overcoming our being wound with his being. Since we were originally created in God's good and perfect image, Jesus comes to recreate this in us. Where the kingdom of God is being manifested, creation is being healed. Christ's life now becomes our life. Out of a vast human community characterized by sin, shame, fear, deception, and addiction, he comes to call a new kind people. The risen, triumphant Lord welcomes us as we are and gives us to each other. Together we are incorporated into his eternal destiny. Now we can become whole again as we begin to share our lives with the only truly functional person who has ever lived this side of the Fall. He alone takes us home to the Father and throws a party.

Part Two

The One Fully
Functional Person

. . .

Chapter 5

Living With
the Fearless Jesus

•   •   •

T he New Testament writers were unanimous in their pre-
sentation of Jesus as the incarnate, sinless Son who is
fully God and fully man. Since he is sinless, he is man-
kind as God created it to be. With this secure theological base,
it isn't mere modernization to present him as also fully functional. The words *functional* and *dysfunctional* can imply an
impersonal and mechanistic worldview. But these terms can
also describe relationships, and relationships are central to the
meaning of life and the Bible's message. When Jesus is called
fully functional, he is authentically human in every way. He
feels, thinks, and says what he means. He's a fully transparent
and integrated person. To come to him is to step onto a path-
way of becoming functional ourselves—in essence becoming
Christlike. And to become like him is to become like his Father.

Jesus restores us to our heavenly Father, overturning the
religion of this addictive, dysfunctional world. As we've seen,
the heart of Jesus' relationship with God was revealed in the
word *Abba*. This expression of intimacy not only showed
something crucial about the Father, it spoke of something crucial in the Son. By using "Abba," Jesus became like a child com-
muning with his Father. As the eternal Son, he was never
abused by a divine poisonous pedagogy. As a result, he was
emotionally free. He had no hole in his soul. He suffered no

being wound and so felt no shame. He always knew perfect love because he lived in a love relationship with his heavenly Father. As Gerald May notes, detachment "does not mean freedom from desire but the freedom of desire."[1] This is what Jesus had—desire, free from all attachments that would keep him from his Father.

As both divine and human, Jesus was the one complete person that has ever lived. He was like the child who, in the words of Alice Miller, was a messenger "from a world we once deeply knew, but which we have long since forgotten, who can reveal to us more about the true secrets of life, and also our own lives, than our parents were ever able to do."[2] Jesus didn't live with repressed feelings that caused him neuroses. His personality was fully integrated. Abuse hadn't curbed his vital spontaneity. He never denied the child within in order to prove that he was a competent adult. Because his own emotions were not shut down, he could respond to other people's pain. Miller observes that those who know their own feelings can only be themselves. She writes,

> Rejection, ostracism, loss of love, and name calling will not fail to affect them; they will suffer as a result and will dread them, but once they have found their authentic self they will not want to lose it. And when they sense that something is being demanded of them to which their whole being says no, they cannot do it.[3]

This explains on a human level Jesus' authenticity and strength.

He not only knew his own feelings, but also constantly knew the Father's love. It's with this insight that Jesus said that all must become as little children in order to enter the kingdom. In doing so we will become like Christ, God will be our "Abba," and we will become functional persons in our own right.

Jesus' security made him absolutely fearless. To live with him, therefore, is to become more and more fearless ourselves.

Jesus Is Fearless in His Identity and Destiny

In the New Testament, Jesus clearly knew who he was. He didn't suffer from an identity crisis. Like Adam and Eve before the Fall, he was "naked and unashamed." In other words, he was utterly transparent. He didn't have a false identity. He always was and always is the eternal Son of God, the express revelation of the Father, the eternal Word—the speech and action of God, going out to create the universe and make the Father known.

Because he was clear about his identity as the Son of God, he lived in intimate communion with his heavenly Father. Since Jesus had never abandoned God, he didn't feel abandoned. There was no divine judgment on his head. He experienced temptation, loneliness, sorrow, and grief as we do, but these experiences came to him while he was fully aware of God's presence. Even from the cross—his darkest moment—while he experienced separation from God, he prayed.

Jesus was not only secure in his identity, but also in his destiny. He intersected our world in order to be Messiah and Savior. He's now the King who brings in God's kingdom, restoring sovereignty over all things. As the Anointed One, he was the Suffering Servant of the Lord who came to close the gap between a holy God and a sinful people. According to John's Gospel, Jesus states that he's bread for our souls; light for our spirits; the door to the Father's presence; the good shepherd who lays down his life for the sheep; the resurrection and the life; the way, the truth, and the life; and the true vine that keeps us green and fruitful. His claim that "no one comes to the Father but by Me" is of ultimate importance.

Jesus makes us secure about our own identity and destiny. When we live with addiction and abuse, we learn and practice addiction and abuse. When we live with Jesus, who is without sin and addiction, we start our recovery. He begins to fill the holes in our souls. A rock musician friend told me, "People said that I should look deeply into myself. I did, and found nothing there. Then I asked Jesus into my life. Now something is there." Like my friend, as we welcome Jesus into our lives, he will be there. Our identity and destiny will be in him.

Jesus shows us that that the image of God, lost in the Fall, is now being restored in us. His character is being manifested in us. We hear and understand his call to follow him as his call to be like him. Jesus tells us, "It is enough for the disciple that he become as his teacher, and the slave as his master" (Matt. 10:25). Paul adds: "But we all, with unveiled face beholding as in a mirror the glory of the Lord, are being transformed into the same image from glory to glory . . ." (2 Cor. 3:18). As God makes us over, it allows us to relax. We are under construction but sure of the outcome. Our identity is to become like Jesus. Our destiny is to be with him forever.

Jesus Is Fearless in His Message and Mission

Since Jesus had a deep inner security about his identity, he was fearless in what he said and did. He beheld the face of the Father, heard what the Father said (John 8:28), saw what the Father did (John 5:19), and acted accordingly. His message was that the Father's kingdom had come. His mission was to do the Father's will. Jesus remains fearless in telling us this message today. He comes bearing divine revelation—his eyes piercing right through us, his words cutting like knives. There is a fire within him that burns into our hearts.

What has Jesus come to tell us? In sum, he announces that the eternal God, enthroned before a sea of angels in endless light, has invaded our space and time to take back his creation from the enemy. God's kingdom is within reach; it's in our midst. Through the power of God, Satan is falling like lightning from heaven (Luke 10:18). Like a strong man who had been bound and his goods stolen, all that he has done to usurp our relationship with God is being reversed.

What God promised in the Old Testament is now being fulfilled. The Davidic Warrior King has come to defeat all his enemies and usher in the new age of peace, prosperity, and security. This Warrior King is also the Suffering Servant of the Lord who, through the cross and empty tomb, defeated the last great enemies of sin and death. Jesus' call to enter the kingdom remains direct and simple. In the Gospels he said all must count the cost; sell all that they have; let the dead bury the dead; put their hands to the plow and not look back; humble themselves and become as little children; and finally, die to themselves and be born again.

Once we've entered the kingdom, we begin to experience God's restored rule. We are free to love him with all of our hearts, souls, minds, and strength. We love our neighbors as ourselves. We love ourselves! By seeking the kingdom of God and his righteousness first, everything else will be added to us. The time will come when our faith will move mountains. With the Word sown in our hearts, we will be part of a gigantic harvest. We will see the kingdom grow from a tiny seed to a great tree as we preach the gospel of the kingdom to all the nations. And then, the end will come; when the cosmos collapses and the holy angels gather us for the judgment, our faces will shine like the sun in God's presence.

Secure in who he is, Jesus fearlessly preaches his message. He tells us the truth about himself and ourselves. All of us can know God and enter his kingdom. Salvation is here. His Spirit is being poured out. It is yes or no, and our eternal destiny, heaven or hell, hangs in the balance.

Jesus was also fearless about his mission. When he set himself against the powers of darkness, demons were cast out, the sick healed, the blind saw, lepers were cleansed, and the dead raised. This kingdom ministry is now ours as well. Like Jesus, we can preach the gospel, heal the sick, and cast out demons.

Jesus' power and authority was also placed in the context of humble service. One of the best examples of his servanthood was when he washed the disciples' feet. His freedom to perform this symbolically menial act came from his authority, produced by his secure relationship with the Father. As John 13:3–5 says,

> Jesus, knowing that the Father had given all things into His hands, and that He had come forth from God, and was going back to God, rose from supper, and laid aside His garments; and taking a towel . . . poured water into the basin, and began to wash the disciples' feet. . . .

This was a person who had a clear sense of himself—he came from God and he was going to God. Out of this self-knowledge his service was neither manipulative nor self-gratifying. Jesus wasn't codependently masking his anger, resentment, and abuse behind his pious good deeds with a towel and basin. His mission came out of pure love. Today, as he bows before us and washes our feet, he breaks our pride in order to heal us.

On the night before my close friend Gary was inducted into the army, he gave me a concrete example of service. As we sat in our living room, reminiscing about the past, he did a curious thing. Getting up, he went into the bathroom and returned with a damp towel and bar of soap. Then, getting on his knees before me, he began to untie my shoes. For a moment, I was confused. Then I thought of Jesus' last night with his disciples. Embarrassment welled up inside me. I wanted to say, "Stop. Don't," but couldn't bring myself to say it. I thought, "My socks are dirty; my feet smell." As I sat there and let Gary wash my feet, my shame and protest passed. I felt instead a profound sense of love and gratitude for this brother. Through Gary's humble act of service, Jesus met me and broke my pride that night.

Living with Jesus will make us like Jesus. As we go through the process of dying daily to our false selves, we will live fearlessly, sharing Jesus' message and mission with others. We will drive to the core issues of their lives with authority and compassion. It won't be our codependent preoccupation to please others. We will truly love them, regardless of the cost. The most loving thing we can do is tell them that Jesus loves them so unconditionally that he calls them into a relationship with himself. Unlike the modern Church, which covers its fear of failure and unbelief in a haze of pluralism, we will be extending God's rule over his enemies and reclaiming planet earth for his kingdom.

I experienced this fearlessness one night when a friend invited me to a Nichiren Shoshu Buddhist meeting. As I sat in a crowded Hollywood living room, several dozen converts and inquirers sang heartily and then listened to a man deliver an enthusiastic message about the benefits of their special Buddhist chant. He said that if we were to join him in chanting, regardless of our personal beliefs, we would get what we wanted. Chanting would automatically align us with the natural force of the universe. "Chant for a car and you will get a car; chant for a girl and you will get a girl," he promised.

Then it was time for questions.

Troubled at the deception and selfishness I sensed from him, I finally raised my hand and asked, "If I were dying of cancer and had five minutes to live, what would you have to say to me?" He avoided the point and answered simply, "We are interested in life. Chant for a car and you will get a car . . ."

Dissatisfied, I raised my hand again. "I don't feel that you addressed my questions. What do you have to say about death?"

He replied, "We talk about life, not death. Anyway, no one has come back from the dead to tell us."

At this point, the truth overpowered my fears. "You're wrong," I answered, "one has come back from the dead. Jesus Christ has told us." With that last remark, the meeting was closed; I was quickly ushered from the room. For that moment the fearless Jesus had spoken his truth through me. I confess that there was joy and relief in my heart as I exited into the night.

Jesus Is Fearless about What He Thinks

To meet Jesus is to know fully functional humanity as God intended it to be. Jesus was the genuine article. Without feeling abandoned or fearful, he had no false self to cover up. He was transparent in his thought life, so he spoke his mind. Being Truth, he always told the truth.

The Gospels show that Jesus was fearlessly truthful with his disciples. He was the charismatic leader who commanded them to leave everything to follow him. With bold confidence he promised to take charge of their lives and make them into "fishers of men." He also wanted to create an inclusive fellowship. Thus he not only spoke the truth, he also acted out the truth. Unafraid of public opinion, he welcomed both Matthew, a hated tax collector and collaborator of Rome, and the political revolutionary, Simon the Zealot, into his inner circle. Women were also drawn into his disciple band, creating great offense in the prevailing Jewish culture. Contradicting rabbinical rules, Jesus invited Mary to sit at his feet and receive instruction as one of his followers.

During the Jesus Movement of the late 1960s, I experienced this kind of inclusive fellowship. During one period, I lived in a house with a seminary student, a drag queen, a drug addict, a patient released from a psychiatric hospital, an illiterate mountain man from Tennessee, a Mormon bishop's son fleeing the law, and a hustler just off the streets. Neither race, culture, nor education brought us together, but we took care of each other because Jesus had called us and made us one. His fearlessness helped take away our reserve and fear of each other. As others came into our house, they saw this sociological miracle. They would ask, "What on earth are you all doing here?" Our only answer was, "Jesus." His truth was not only preached, it was seen in us. Even though at that time I didn't know all that I needed in order to be healed, Jesus was already working in me!

Jesus' inclusive fellowship was also functional because he wasn't a people pleaser. He expects as much from us today. Our outward action must reflect our inward motivation. This honesty is our "exceeding righteousness" (Matt. 5:20). When he told people not to harbor anger or lust in their hearts, he was expressing interest in motivation rather than in confused and deceptive behavior. No wonder he warned against those who managed impressions and were preoccupied with image and lifestyle. He called them actors and hypocrites. When we are living with Jesus, no one has to second guess him or us. Freed from codependency and deception, our yes means yes and our no means no.

Since Jesus had no fear, he dealt honestly and directly with his disciples (and with us, he is both honest and direct). Unlike our addictive and codependent culture, he never shied away from confrontation. He never "triangulated," asking James or John to tell Judas something for him. When Peter sought to block him from suffering in Jerusalem, Jesus commanded, "Get behind me Satan . . . you are not setting your mind on God's interests, but man's" (Matt. 16:23).

Jesus was truthful with his disciples because he knew their hearts. He knew they were self-serving. He knew their attachments, their pride, their schemes for power positions. He also knew their fears for the future and prophetically prepared himself for their denial and treachery. Moreover, Jesus knew how little they understood the supernatural world in which he lived and fearlessly rebuked their unbelief. Through these honest rebuffs, the hearts of his followers were exposed. Nevertheless, he loved them to the end. Jesus revealed that mercy and grace were greater than buried deception and pride.

With unequaled vision, Jesus saw beyond the disciples' masks and the false selves that covered their abandonment and shame. Because of Jesus, Simon became Peter, the Rock. This name change expressed the new identity that Jesus would give to all. Jesus was unafraid to call people to go with him, deny themselves and their addictive attachments, become outcasts, and take up the cross with him. Only by dying to their old lives and completely abandoning everything to him would they continue to enjoy his fellowship and share in his destiny.

Jesus still wants to make disciples like the twelve. In order to create true followers, he promises to bring us to repentance over our idols, deliver us from addictions, restore our abused inner child, reawaken our sleeping emotions, and make us real, inside and out. In Jesus' plan for the modern Church, "What you see is what you get." Politics and game playing are over. The truth is made incarnate through us.

I witnessed this type of deliverance at a Christmas party in a former church. I was having a superficial conversation with an elder, when a thought suddenly flashed into my mind. Before I could stop myself, I asked, "Are you having an affair?" Shocked at my own question, I was more shocked by his reply. "Yes," he confessed, "I am." Even more miraculous, he had been praying for two weeks for the courage to admit the affair to someone. That night God answered his prayer through me. The exposure of his secret burden led to repentance, account-ability, and healing. The Church was no longer a safe place for compulsive, deceptive sin. Jesus' truth penetrated the darkness and made us real.

Jesus was not only fearless with his disciples, he also fear-lessly told the truth to the multitudes. He had come to seek and save the lost. It was the common people, the poor, the sick, and the oppressed who were the objects of his love. Rather than shrink back from a raving demoniac, a putrid wound, or a maimed body, Jesus was drawn toward these very things. He refused to live in denial about the pain he saw. There was nothing self-protective in his nature.

Like the good shepherd, Jesus looked for his one lost sheep. At Simon the Pharisee's dinner party, his mercy reached out to a prostitute who washed his feet with her tears. In spite of his offended host, Jesus justified and welcomed her affection, "I say to you, her sins, which are many, have been forgiven, for she loved much . . ." (Luke 7:47). He showed mercy to the hated Samaritan woman who had had five ex-husbands and a current live-in lover. Unafraid of public opinion regarding the Mosaic law, he refused to condemn a woman taken in the very act of adultery. Later, he called the despised tax collector Zacchias down from the limb of a tree. He announced to his startled hearers that he would have dinner at Zacchias's house and bring salvation to him.

Jesus' fearlessness in speaking the truth was again apparent when he gave an ultimatum to a rich young ruler looking for eternal life. Knowing that his attachment to money would keep him from the kingdom, Jesus told him to sell all he had, give it to the poor, and then come follow him. Only through detaching himself could the ruler have treasure in heaven. When the man turned sorrowfully away, Jesus was compassionate, yet refused to withdraw or change his terms. He hadn't asked him to become religious. In love, he sought to liberate the ruler without violating his will. Jesus' call was clear and the cost radical. The man made his choice. Jesus honored his decision.

When Jesus talked to Nicodemus, an important Pharisee, he was not misled by flattery or praise. He came right to the point when he told Nicodemus that he had to be "born again." In other words, this sophisticated leader of Israel had to become like a little child, entering a new spiritual world like a baby. Jesus wasn't afraid to drive the truth home. Nicodemus had to be humbled to come into the kingdom. He couldn't keep his pride and position. This was confrontational love. Here is the truth that will set us free.

During the course of my ministry, I've witnessed Jesus continuing to reach out to multitudes of sick and broken people. I recall meeting Carol, who was pregnant and thrown out by her mother, drifting from man to man on the Sunset Strip. Out of desperation, she found her way to the largest church in Hollywood, hoping to be lost in the crowd. After the message struck her, she waited for me with mascara running down her cheeks. We sat down to talk. She rehearsed her story and ended with a natural comment, "God could never forgive me. I'm too bad." With this admission I knew that she wasn't far from the kingdom. I shared the simple message of Jesus' love and forgiveness. Within twenty minutes Carol received the fearless Christ who told her who she was and without apology loved her into his arms.

I remember talking to Biff about Jesus on the front lawn of the house where I was staying in Wichita. As his objections to Christianity melted, I saw in his eyes that the moment had come to pray. I hesitated because he had a live-in girlfriend. I wondered, "Should I bring her up?" What if I lost him at this point? Jesus, though, wouldn't let me off the hook. I felt conviction overcoming my fears and said, "Before we pray, I have to ask you about your relationship with your lover." I'll never forget Biff's answer, "If I trusted someone who loved me, and they would tell me what to do, I would do it." With this reply, I knew he was ready to ask Jesus into his life. He did and within a day moved out of his living situation. Two months later his girlfriend became a Christian, and shortly after they were married. Like Nicodemus, Biff experienced Jesus' confrontational love, and the truth set him free.

Jesus was just as fearlessly truthful to his enemies. He battled with the devil in the wilderness and won by the truth of God's Word. He confronted demons by pulling off their covers. He stared them down, bringing them to heel by the naked authority of his command. Mark 1:25 states that when his teaching was interrupted by a possessed man, he said to the dark spirit, "Be quiet and come out of him." Later he found the crazed demoniac, Legion, living naked and mutilated among the tombs. Jesus exposed the hosts of evil inhabiting his body and ordered them to go. As they fled, the man was set free.

Jesus' most consistent opponents were the religious elders and teachers of Israel. In Matthew 23:27 he called them hypocrites, "white washed tombs, full of dead men's bones." He accused them of practicing their piety in order to be seen. They prayed long prayers to the watching galleries. When they fasted, they wore gaunt faces to impress others. They sought honor by positioning themselves at the heads of the tables. Their religious pretention made them and their proselytes children of hell.

Jesus had little to do with the political state. When he did confront the powers of justice, he was marvelously, truthfully consistent. Throwing caution to the wind, he identified Herod as a sly fox. Later, when his life hung in the balance, he told Pilate that Caesar's power came from the God of Israel.

The fearless Christ continues to confront his enemies with the truth today. I knew a woman who had been trained as a medium by her grandmother and aunt. She held numberless seances. After she became a Christian, she was still plagued by the remnants of her past. In one instance, she tried to burn herself to death. A fellow pastor brought her to me for prayer. She renounced all the occult practices in which she had been involved. The pastor and I proceeded to break curses and hexes that had been placed on her by her family. At one point I asked her to name the spirits that had communicated with her during her seances. One by one I ordered them out of her in Jesus' name. As the final one left, it literally hurled her across the room. As the demon exploded out of her, she was set free for the first time in her life. These deceptive enemies were again brought down with the authority of Jesus' name.

Because Jesus is fearless, he always tells the truth. He speaks his mind. He has nothing to hide. We may love or hate what he's saying, but we must admit that in contrast to our addictive culture and Church, he is refreshing. As the world's one fully functional person, Jesus tells us what he thinks and feels.

Jesus Is Fearless in What He Feels

Unlike a dysfunctional person, Jesus knew what he felt. His central teaching was to love God with everything and love our neighbors as ourselves. When the rich young ruler came to Jesus, Mark 10:21 tells us, "And looking at him, Jesus felt a love for him. . . ." John 11:5 says that Jesus ". . . loved Martha, and her sister, and Lazarus." The special relationship Jesus had with John is seen when John reclines on Jesus' breast at the Last Supper. He was known as the disciple "whom Jesus loved" (John 21:7).

The emotion of Jesus' love was clearly expressed by his compassion toward the lost. In Greek, the word for *compassion* means "to feel something in the inward parts or the center of emotion." So, in Matthew 9:36, Jesus feels with his full emotions: "And seeing the multitudes, He felt compassion for them, because they were distressed and downcast like sheep without a shepherd." It is out of compassion that he fed the five thousand with a few loaves and fishes. The blind saw and a widow's dead son was raised to life because Jesus was moved with compassion.

In Luke 19:41–44, his compassion was mixed with grief when he wept over his prophetic vision of Jerusalem in ruins:

And when He approached, He saw the city and wept over it, saying "If you had known in this day, even you, the things which make for peace! But now they have been hidden from your eyes. For the days shall come upon you when your enemies will throw up a bank before you, and surround you, and hem you in on every side, and will level you to the ground and your children within you. . . ."

Jesus experienced grief when he wept before Lazarus's tomb. The fact that he would shortly raise him from the dead in no way inhibited his feeling of pathos.

As Jesus faced the cross, his heart was troubled and tormented. His distress in the garden of Gethsemene led him to wonder whether he should ask God to save him from his hour. His battle in Gethsemene was a real battle, and his cry of anguish from the cross was a real cry. Jesus wasn't a stoic philosopher. Death is a real enemy, and he was fully human before it.

Jesus also felt and expressed anger. He was angered and grieved at the hardness of the Pharisees' hearts when they judged him for healing on the Sabbath. His wrath rose up when he saw corruption in the temple. He responded by driving out the money changers who made profits from the worship of God. Like God's wrath, his anger was always moral. Since it was directed at sin and its consequences, it was never self-serving.

Jesus was not only acquainted with sorrows and grief and consumed with righteous indignation, he was also a man of great joy.

Jesus' joy was found, first of all, in his relationship with his heavenly Father. After his disciples returned from casting out demons, Luke 10:21 records: "At that very time He rejoiced greatly in the Holy Spirit, and said, 'I praise Thee, O Father, Lord of heaven and earth, that Thou didst hide these things from the wise and intelligent and didst reveal them to babes. Yes, Father, for thus it was well-pleasing in Thy sight.'" Jesus expressed his own joy at the lost being found through the story of the shepherd. When the shepherd found his stray lamb, he placed it on his shoulders with rejoicing. In the parable of the prodigal son, the father expressed joy at the return of the prodigal by throwing a party. No wonder Jesus told his disciples,

"These things I have spoken to you, that My joy may be in you, and that your joy may be made full" (John 15:11).

As we grow in fellowship with the real Jesus, he will fearlessly deal with us. He will us secure in his great love. As he exposes our sins and reveals our emotional wounds and generational bondages, he will heal us. He will break down our walls of fear and break up our hard hearts. He will overcome our shame base and heal our being wound through his presence and grace. This means that denial, avoidance, and repression will not work for us. He will always tell us the truth, and that truth will set us free. It is Jesus' intention to turn us into fearless people. He wants us to join him in confronting the confusion, deception, and lies of this world. Now and forever we will no longer be alone. As Paul says, "If God is for us, who can be against us?" (Rom. 8:31). Nothing can separate us from his love.

Chapter 6

Living With
the Free Jesus

.   .   .

Billy had bloodshot eyes, a bloated face, scraggly hair, and open sores. He lived in an alley near my office where I often encountered him. His rage made him passive aggressive, but he had a tender heart. He was an alcoholic and very sick. He had seizures that often landed him in the hospital until finally an infection killed him. A freeway ramp carried his spray-painted memorial. To his friends he was a cosmic king. Billy was free from family, work, responsibility, and any commitment beyond himself. But was he really free?

The humanist assumes that to be free is to do whatever one pleases. If people's reason is clear and their will is free, their only limitations are physical. The Marxist assumes just the opposite. People are in bondage, personally, intellectually, and morally to economic forces beyond their control. Freedom is simply participation in a new collective political consciousness and the inevitable historical process taking them to a classless utopia. The Freudian contends that people are prisoners of the unconscious drives of love and death. Freedom can only be gained by becoming conscious of the wishes and needs that control them in order to adjust to the daily pain of life.

From the study of addiction, however, it's clear that everyone is in bondage. For us there is no "natural" freedom. Only when God's grace intervenes in our lives and we die and are raised with Christ can we progressively detach ourselves from all the things that had controlled us. Rather than the bondage of desire, we increasingly experience the freedom of true desire. This freedom means that we will not turn any substance, process, or relationship into an idol, losing control to anything outside the control of God. This freedom means that we are now able to think, say, and feel truthfully without fear of abandonment or shame. This freedom means that down deep in our guts we know that we are loved unconditionally by Jesus and are secure in him for eternity.

As a result, we can at last love God with all our hearts, souls, and minds, and love our neighbors as ourselves.

How can we nurture this new freedom? How can we prevent relapse into addiction and codependency? First, we must live with Jesus, the only fully free person on this planet, day by day. As we experience his freedom, we will be set free from our attachments, compulsions, and addictions.

It's a paradox to speak of Jesus' freedom. On one hand, he absolutely submitted to the Father. On the other hand, since this submission came out of love, he was absolutely free. Jesus' love for the Father came from the Father. It was self-giving love. In John 17:21 he prayed, ". . . for Thou didst love Me before the foundation of the world." Out of his response to this unconditional love, he spoke what the Father spoke and did what the Father did. In this way he fulfilled his destiny.

Jesus' freedom was grounded in his identity with the Father. He was never insecure about the Father's love for him. His Father never abusively withheld love for Jesus' own good. Jesus never taught the truth or healed diseases with one eye on the Father, anxiously watching to see if God was cheering from the grandstands. He wasn't trying to win the approval of the Father or other people.

Jesus said that all he did came as a gift from the Father's heart. Jesus found his freedom in open communion with God, serving as a channel for what the Father wanted to accomplish.

Consequently, Jesus was free from any external code. He had no need to check out how people felt about him in order to know how he felt about himself.

Unlike addictive and codependent people, Jesus had no illusion that he could control everything. Because he was submitted to his Father, he didn't have to get control of himself. This made him free from seeking to control circumstances or people. Fear of failure, exposure, or of losing his addictive fix weren't hooks for him. Since Jesus was certain of who he was, he was free from the bondage of human control and expectations. Instead he was free to love, confront, comfort, heal, and save people.

Through Jesus' example, we learn that freedom isn't found in autonomy or separation from God. Real freedom is found in unity and communion with God. No wonder Jesus says that apart from himself we can do nothing. God made us for relationship and rulership. To exercise our inherent relationship with God is to be the free people we were created to be. To understand Jesus' freedom more specifically and to begin to emulate it (through his Spirit), let's look at both the negative side and the positive side of his freedom.

What Is Jesus Free From?

First of all, Jesus was free from bondage to the devil. Because of this, he exposed Satan as a murderer from the beginning. All death wishes, suicidal compulsions, and violence toward God's creation reflect Satan's hostility toward the God who both orders life and offers eternal life through his Son. Jesus said Satan was a liar and the father of lies. He is the ultimate source of all deception. Into this death and darkness, Jesus spoke the truth that sets us free today.

Because he was free, Jesus ransacked Satan's kingdom. He broke the control of afflicting spirits and ordered them out.

Often such power encounters came with incredible force, throwing people into convulsions as the shrieking devils left. Physical and emotional healing resulted. A woman demonically bent over for eighteen years was straightened. Jesus found Legion, a man hosting an army of demons, and left him clothed and in his right mind.

When we begin to live with Jesus we will be increasingly free from Satan. We won't be ignorant of his schemes. We will be able to discern the presence of his evil spirits. Any demons who have hooked themselves into us will have to leave. Whether they leave at the time of our conversion, or some time later by renunciation and repentance, we can withdraw the welcome mat and order them out in Jesus' name.

Tim, a cocaine addict, was set free from several demons who had entered his life through childhood abuse and, later, ten years of drug abuse. A psychologist friend Joe Ozawa and I prayed for him one night and the malignant spirits left. The next day he was free from his moment by moment compulsion to do coke. He has now been clean and sober for several years.

Sadly, Christians may relapse into satanic bondage and need to be set free again. Paul exhorted the Ephesians to give no opportunity or handle to the devil. Christians can't live in paranoia, though. They must live in the knowledge that if they resist the devil in Jesus' mighty name, the devil will flee from them.

Jesus also lived free from bondage to this fallen world. As the King who came to inaugurate the kingdom of God, he challenged all other earthly kingdoms. This included the often idolatrous kingdom of the family. While Jesus' parents had a sense of his unique destiny, Jesus nevertheless made an early break from them in submission to a greater authority. At the age of twelve he vanished from his parents' traveling party to return to the temple in Jerusalem and debate with the scribes. When Mary and Joseph found him and challenged his behavior, he responded that he must be about his heavenly Father's business. He later abandoned Joseph's trade in order to begin his messianic ministry. This made the home folks of Nazareth angry at what they supposed was his pretension. Since familiarity breeds contempt, they continued to disparage him. As a result, he didn't do mighty works in their midst. His immediate family couldn't accept his wild apocalyptic teaching. They suspected he had gone mad, and wanted to take him into custody.

It's no wonder that Jesus said in Mark 3:35: "Whoever does the will of God, he is my brother and sister and mother." Free from Jewish family culture he warned in Luke 14:26: "If anyone comes to Me, and does not hate his own father and mother and wife and children and brothers and sisters, yes, and even his own life, he cannot be my disciple." In this passage Jesus demanded that people make a radical break from their pasts in order to find their individual spirituality in him. Today, we must allow Jesus to create clear moral and psychological boundaries. Enraged at losing control of us, our families may become our enemies. In Matthew 10:21–22, Jesus warned, "And brother will deliver up brother to death, and a father his child; and children will rise up against parents, and cause them to be put to death. And you will be hated by all on account of My name."

This violence is the result of shame from the Fall that has been transmitted to us by our parents. They then use this inbred shame to bind us with their judgments. Their demands are enforced by the controls of conditional love and withheld approval. This shuts down our inner child and leaves us emotionally and spiritually broken. Our symbolic death can include actual ostracism by some natural families. I remember a young women who was threatened with disinheritance by her wealthy family if she continued in her faith. Such pressure has made her live far from home but catapulted her into spiritual maturity.

Jesus was also free from the kingdom of religious legalism, which still produces fake pride and encourages practices that debilitate the Church and people's lives. (This is what authors

Stephen Arterburn and Jack Felton call "toxic faith.") Legalism entraps people in perfectionism and performance. Caught in this, they live outside of themselves, fearful of what others may think. They hide behind the false self of religious piety, seeking their own self-justification. Addicted to institutional approval and control, their guilt is only relieved by all the things they do. In essence, they are practicing righteousness in order to be noticed by people. Jesus warned of such behavior when he spoke against the hypocritical clergy who said things but didn't do them. He also warned of those Pharisees who looked good but were addicted to their own self-image. It's grace and grace alone that will free us from such religious performance. Jesus modeled this for us and gives it to us now in full measure.

Jesus was free from the kingdom of economic bondage—bondage to the fear of losing things and of scarcity. As a celibate, itinerant evangelist, his needs were simple. He knew that his heavenly Father would take care of him. Having no permanent place to lay his head, he relied on the graciousness of others. Consistent with his own poverty, he warned that the idolatry and oppression of riches made it hard for a wealthy man to enter the kingdom of God. Even while most of his followers raised families, owned property, and lived settled lives, they, like Jesus, couldn't serve both God and money. It was not only Jesus' intention to attack the idol of materialism for his generation, but to deliver us from a similar bondage to money today. This deliverance promises us that our heavenly Father will clothe us like the lilies of the field and watch over us like a hawk. If we seek God's kingdom and righteousness first, all else will follow. Like the disciples, most of us will marry and have earthly possessions, but we will enjoy the same care the Father lavished on Jesus.

Jesus is free from the kingdom of this world system with its false values of power, pride of position, and control. He is free from its demands of performance for acceptance. As we have seen, in the religious world this includes praying long prayers in the marketplace, fasting with a drawn face, seeking the chief seat in church, and parading piety before people.

Since Jesus is free from all of this, he can set us free as well. Transparency and truth are his weapons, exposing the lies of our lives. Thus every idol must go. Every attachment must be broken. Jesus is relentless. He wants it all and will have it all. This fallen world has no claim on him, and it is to have no claim on us. He is Lord.

Jesus was also free from the bondage of sin. The New Testament authors made it clear that he was the sinless Son of God. While the Gospels continually display him as a man of utter humility, they never show him asking God for forgiveness. In fact, he had the audacity to forgive the sins of others. C. S. Lewis pointed out that Christ assumed that all evil deeds were ultimately committed against himself,[1] a position that had been held by God alone.

The Gospel writers revealed another aspect of Jesus' sinlessness; he continually did the will of the Father. Only out of perfect communion could he have said, "The words that I say to you I do not speak on my own initiative, but the Father abiding in me does His works. Believe Me that I am in the Father, and the Father in Me" (John 14:10–11). John 17:4 helps provide raw material for the doctrine of sinlessness when Jesus prayed in the garden of Gethsemene, "I glorified Thee on the earth, having accomplished the work which Thou hast given me to do." Paul wrote, "[God] made Him who knew no sin to be sin on our behalf, that we might become the righteousness of God in Him" (2 Cor. 5:21). Peter adds, "Christ also suffered for you . . . who committed no sin, nor was any deceit found in His mouth" (1 Pet. 2:22).

The heart of the Gospel is that the sinless Jesus takes our sins on himself and in return gives us forgiveness and freedom. Our release from sin comes by his words of forgiveness and final act of forgiveness on the cross. We gain ownership of this forgiveness when we humble ourselves, repent, and confess our sins. With clean hearts, a new freedom can now be ours.

Since Jesus was sinless, he was free from the bondage of Law. He could keep the whole law effortlessly; "Do not think that I came to abolish the Law or the Prophets; I did not come to abolish, but to fulfill" (Matt. 5:17). Because Jesus lived in complete communion with his Father, his obedience to the law wasn't religious. It came spontaneously from his heart.

It's from this perspective that he taught in Matthew 5:48, "you are to be perfect, as your heavenly Father is perfect." This demand drives us to despair. How can we burn with the same moral purity as God? But after despair becomes admission that we are powerless over our lives, it drives us to Jesus. He is the perfect one and we can only be perfect in him. Our obedience to the law now comes from his gift of grace. Dietrich Bonhoeffer taught that before we come to Christ we have a direct relationship to the law. Its demands are fully laid on us. When we come to Christ, however, we have an indirect relationship to the law. We only relate to it through Christ, who acts as our mediator. Jesus added only one thing to the law: He kept it and thereby fulfilled it in himself.[2] Now we can keep it and fulfill it through him.

Finally, Jesus was free from the bondage of the flesh. This base nature, manifested in futile self-reliance, results in the corruption of all our desires through addictive attachments. Jesus didn't live strictly for himself but rather in complete dependence on the Father. He gave himself away out of his secure sense of identity and destiny. Rather than meeting his own needs, as we are manipulated to do by our consumer culture, he came to do his Father's will by freely meeting the needs of others.

Empowered by the Spirit after his baptism, he fulfilled his messianic ministry free from fleshly fallen nature. He promised that this same life is possible for us, if we die to ourselves, receive his resurrected life, and become filled with the Spirit.

What Is Jesus Free For?

In Jesus we see humanity as it was intended to be—free. But freedom isn't just being released from Satan, the world, sin, the law, and the flesh. We are set free for God and for each other.

In John's Gospel, Jesus said that his obedience showed the world that he loved the Father. Because of his love, he withdrew to a lonely place in the early hours of the morning to be in God's presence. His intimacy with the Father was sustained out of his love. It is was out of this same love and intimacy that Jesus ministered. His resulting works only served to bear witness to the fact that the Father had sent him.

Knowledge and love of the Father, however, meant that Jesus wasn't addicted to his ministry or relationships. Unlike today's pastoral workaholics, he was free to leave a successful campaign behind and move on to other cities. Since he was motivated by God's call rather than by the needs around him, he was free to withdraw from the masses and find rest and refreshment without guilt.

The will of God is fulfilled in two Old Testament commands. In Matthew 22:37–40, when an expert of the law asked Jesus about the great commandment, Jesus responded, "'You shall love the Lord your God with all your heart, and with all your soul, and with all your mind.' This is the great and foremost commandment. The second is like it, 'You shall love your neighbor as yourself.' On these two commandments depend the whole Law and the Prophets." It is for this that Jesus was free. He was free to love God fully and he is free to love us in the same way.

As we grow in our relationship with Jesus, we will grow in our love for God. The first commandment won't be our burden but our delight. Like Jesus, we will seek the Father's face and express our love for him in worship and growing intimacy. Like Jesus we will listen for God's Word and do his will. As we travel with Jesus our love for him will reveal our love for the Father.

Since Jesus loved people from wholeness, he had no addictively attaching relationships. Unlike many pastors today, he didn't need to collect important people around him in order to shore up his fragile ego. (He must be unimpressed with our obsession over gathering wealthy, powerful people for our church boards. He would have needed no endorsements from rock stars, Nobel Prize winners, athletes, or political leaders.)

Being free from people, Jesus was free for people. Common folk gladly listened to him. He could relate to fishermen, revolutionaries, soldiers, and slaves. When he went to the home of a Pharisee, he didn't have a problem if he met up with a prostitute there. (What would the reaction in church be if any of us arranged to talk with a call girl and asked her to meet us at a local bishop's dinner party?) He loved to eat with tax collectors and sinners. In Luke 7:36 his enemies accused him of being a "gluttonous man, and a drunkard." Unlike the Pharisees, he didn't avoid traveling through the hated and defiled region of Samaria. Although he had been sent to the lost sheep of Israel, occasionally he lavished his love on the defiled Gentiles. Tempting scandal, he welcomed women as his disciples. He also embraced little children, taking them in his arms and blessing them as signs of the kingdom. Farmers, shepherds, babies— these humble people provided the images for many of his sayings and parables.

Jesus was completely free to care for all kinds of people. He confronted them, responded to their pain, and was just there for them. I once heard Dick Halverson, Chaplain of the U.S. Senate, remark, "Jesus could not be interrupted since his ministry was his interruptions. His agenda was to identify human need and do what love dictates." When Jesus responds to us, he goes beyond the conscious things that usually force us to seek help such as alcoholism or chronic depression. By confronting the core issues of our lives, he risks rejection. When he walked the earth, the freedom and well-being of those around him were his greatest values. For this reason, he continued to love a world that responded to him with hatred. When he said "love your enemies" (Matt. 5:44), he could be believed, for he signed this demand in his own blood.

Because of this fallen world's hostility and Israel's expectations of a politically powerful Messiah, Jesus knew that he would experience tremendous suffering. He actually viewed himself as bringing division and conflict. His disciples misunderstood him. His opponents hounded him and plotted his death. Judas betrayed him. Peter denied him. Finally, Jesus laid his naked body down on Roman boards and allowed himself to be nailed between heaven and earth. He asked his heavenly Father to forgive his enemies and in return was left to bleed and suffocate to death. Such love breaks our pride and our hearts. But we must understand that it's through such suffering that Christ's kingdom fully comes.

This act was the ultimate expression of Jesus' freedom to love his neighbor as himself. All of his acts were acts of love. It was for love that he healed the sick and cast out demons. Love drove him to set us free from the ravages of Satan and sin. It would be exhausting to recount every instance of Jesus' love for people in the Gospels; it's written on every page.

Jesus not only freely loves us, he sets us free to love ourselves and each other. As we receive his mercy and become merciful toward ourselves, we will be able to extend it to our neighbors. Such love throws Christians into each others arms for care and comfort and enables us to bear the good news of Jesus' love into the world. Since he doesn't condemn us, we won't condemn ourselves or each other. Since he loved his enemies, we will love our enemies (even when that enemy may be our abusive selves). Since he forgives us, we will forgive ourselves and each other. Since he comes to seek and save the lost, we will go to seek and save the lost. The great commission will be fulfilled throughout the whole global village by a Church in love with God and its neighbors. As the Church mirrors the presence of Jesus in its midst, it will live out its new freedom in relationship to the only fully functional person who ever lived.

I've been privileged to see the true Church in action. I remember when Jimmy found his way off the streets and into our storefront in San Diego. As he sat in the back, he witnessed Emile, the manager, and his roommate David, say good-bye to Oscar, a black man who had been living with them for a time. As these three grown men parted, they were overcome with Jesus' love. Watching them embrace and weep, Jimmy said to himself, "That's what I want." A short time afterward he became a Christian.

My friend and coworker Jay Hoehn spends a significant time among the homeless in the Mission Beach area of San Diego. One night he was hanging out on the Boardwalk when he spotted a young man vomiting over the wall next to the beach. Jay went over to him and little by little shared the love of Jesus with him. Separated from his friends, this guy had ended up drunk and sick. Jay stayed with him until his friends finally spotted him. As the young man turned to go with them, he swung around and gave Jay a big hug of thanks, saying, "I'll never forget what you told me tonight." As he left, Jay saw that this man's hug had left his own shirt covered with vomit. For me, this is a parable of Jesus' love. When he embraces us, he takes our vomit on himself, while we go free.

To know the free Jesus is to experience our own freedom. It's to be invaded by his Spirit and live an increasingly spontaneous Spirit-led life. To know Jesus is to renounce our idols of relationships, processes, and substances, becoming detached from the addictions that enslave us. To know Jesus is to be liberated from the performance demands of our addictive culture. It is to experience heavenly control (our freedom) rather than earthly control (bondage), even when earthly control is masked by the devil's deceptions, family expectations, or the demands of this world system.

After our relationship with God is restored and we love him with all our hearts, our relationships with each other will be restored. Out of our new relationship with God, we will also be able to exercise rulership over this planet. Sin, Satan, disease, and death will be challenged and conquered in the name of Jesus. While we can only see a partial victory now, we can rest in the assurance that Jesus has already won the battle. We have read the last chapter in the history of time and everything turns out all right. This knowledge makes us spiritually free to be relevant to the world at the deepest level of its hunger—a hunger for the living God.

Chapter 7

Living With
the Self-Giving Jesus

· · ·

A ddicts are either users of substances (drugs, alcohol, nicotine, or caffeine), of people through dysfunctional relationships, or of processes (such as work, gambling, or exercise). They are preoccupied with controlling their addictive source of supply. Because their disease is progressive, they demand more and more of their mood altering substances, activities, or relationships. There is no one as self-centered as an addict in need of a fix.

Jesus is the alternative to an addictive and consumptive life. He was self-giving rather than selfish. Like him Luther called us to live *extra nos*, outside of ourselves, loving God and loving people.

Jesus, however, didn't live outside of himself at the expense of his true thoughts and feelings. He didn't use focusing outside himself as a way to hide his shame. He didn't manipulate people in order to gain control over them, using love to mask rage. He didn't stop living his own life in order to live someone else's life.

Jesus was not a codependent care giver who lost himself serving people out of his own low self-esteem. As Melody Beattie writes, "However you approach codependency, however you define it, and from whatever frame of reference you choose to diagnose and treat it, codependency is primarily a reactionary process. Codependents are reactionaries. They overreact. But rarely do they act."[1] This was not Jesus. He was no victim. He experienced no abandonment so he was naked and unashamed before others. He knew who he was and what he was about.

Secure in his relationship with the Father and in himself as the Son of God, he was free to give himself to others. A friend told me that the psychologist Carl Rogers once counseled, "Get yourself together and give yourself away." As the one true functional person, Jesus was always together. Out of this wholeness, he fearlessly and freely gave himself away.

The Self-Giving Jesus Loves Us

Jesus showed his self-giving nature by loving others. He fully understood that love is a verb as well as a noun; it leads to action. In Luke 10:25–37, Jesus used the parable of the good Samaritan to illustrate this. The story established the meaning of the second great commandment: "You shall love your neighbor as yourself." In the tale, religious leaders traveling on the treacherous Jericho road passed by a man who had been beaten and robbed. They didn't want to get involved. Fearing contamination, they avoided the poor devil. Their speech must have been rife with rationalizations: "I'm late for temple. When I get to Jerusalem I'll demand more police protection for this highway. What a fool to travel alone. This man got what he deserved; he must have some secret sin in his life; I'm glad God judged him."

Surprisingly, while the professional religious leaders avoided the injured man, the hated heretical and half-breed Samaritan stopped. Taking the initiative, he came to where the man was. (We can see that love makes the first move.) Rather than catching an image of the man out of his peripheral vision, the Samaritan actually saw him. (Love doesn't avoid; love doesn't go into denial. Love sees the crisis for what it is. Love faces the truth.) From this honest confrontation, Jesus told us, the Samaritan had compassion—his heart was touched. He paid attention to his initial emotional response and went with his gut reaction. (Notice that this emotion came after he saw the victim. In other words, he wasn't led by his feelings.)

Now we can see love in action. First, the Samaritan took care of the man's wounds and stopped the bleeding. He didn't give a sermon; he gave first aid. Second, he put the man on his donkey and took him to an inn. There he promised the proprietor that he would cover the bill. The Samaritan accepted responsibility for the man's recovery. Jesus concluded that this was what it meant to love our neighbors as ourselves. Christians are to go and do likewise.

For us, the good Samaritan is Jesus. When all others pass us by on the other side of the road, he stops. When no one will give us a glance, he moves toward us and sees our need. He feels compassion. He binds up our wounds and restores us to health. This is Jesus' brand of love—unconditional concern for our best interests without any reference to himself and his needs. He doesn't derive value from us; he invests value in us by loving us. No wonder Jesus was willing to go freely to the cross and die. He never asked, "What's in it for me?" His only concerns were "What's in it for you, Father, and what's in it for them?"

Jesus served his disciples in exactly this way. During Passover, he laid aside his garments and his glory as he washed their feet. Jesus not only loved them, he called them to love each other. He reminded them that they called him Master and Lord, but he would only be their Master and Lord if they did what he did. If he washed their feet, they were to wash one anothers' feet. That footwashing business would be the acid test by which the world would know that the disciples knew him. This was the sign of their discipleship, and it must be the sign of ours.

Jesus gave us examples of how are we could live out this self-givingness: sharing our goods with those in need, caring for those who are poor and oppressed, and laying down our lives for each other. Loving like this is, in the phrase of Reinhold

Niebuhr, our "impossible possibility." Only the love of Jesus can enable us to love each other this way. In John 17:26 he prayed "that the love wherewith Thou didst love Me may be in them, and I in them." Such servantlike love is radical and will always be contrary to the world's standards.

I recall Richard who came to our church from Hollywood Boulevard. He was a large, unattractive, fearful man. He came on sexually to one of our members and, when his overtures weren't returned, he threatened violence. As I got to know Richard, I learned that at a young age he had watched his father shoot his mother and then kill himself. He was then bounced from institution to institution. He finally landed in Hollywood where he came to know Jesus. He received the gift of a simple faith; if it was in the Bible, he believed it. Little by little leaders of the church rallied to help Richard. Bob Toms, who was the governor's Commissioner of Corporations at that time, became his lawyer, working gratis when a landlord threatened to put Richard on the street. Jim Oraker, a psychologist friend of mine, became his counselor and helped him handle his rage. When he contracted hepatitis, it seemed like an army was there with food and cheer.

One night a group of us celebrated Richard's birthday in our living room. As we all stood together holding hands and praying, tears came to my eyes. I looked around the room filled with outstanding, responsible leaders of our community and church who had gathered to honor Richard. In them I saw something of the servantlike heart of Jesus. As Jesus said in Mark 10:42–44,

> You know that those who are recognized as rulers of the Gentiles lord it over them; and their great men exercise authority over them. But it is not so among you, but whoever wishes to become great among you shall be your servant; and whoever wishes to be first among you shall be slave to all.

Why must we be servants? Because "the Son of Man did not come to be served, but to serve, and to give His life a ransom for many" (Mark 10:45). In ministry there may not be much room at the top, but there's always room at the bottom. No one competed with Mother Teresa when she began caring for the dying on the streets of Calcutta. Just as Jesus gave his life for us, he commands us now to go and do likewise.

Jesus not only served his disciples but also served the world. Such service is illustrated compellingly throughout the Gospel narratives. There he lavished his love and power on the demonized, the blind, the lame, the deaf and dumb, the paralyzed, and the lepers. He loved those with withered limbs and withered souls. His hands were always outstretched, touching the untouchables. He heard the cries of the sick and dying and answered them.

It was this kind of love that hooked me as an insecure high school sophomore. I was trapped within myself and fearful of people. I met some Christian school leaders who learned my name and took time for me. They gave me rides to a Tuesday night fellowship that met in area homes. They included me in their fun even though I wasn't any fun. They invited me to a weekend camp where I was directly confronted with the Gospel. When I heard that Jesus loved me unconditionally, I could believe it, because I had already seen this love through their lives.

To live with the self-giving Jesus will mean that we must give ourselves in love to each other and to the world. There really is no option. As we get out of ourselves and get into him and each other, we will learn how to live.

The Self-Giving Jesus Tells Us the Truth

The self-giving Jesus not only shows us his love, but also tells us the truth. In an age of propaganda, image manipulation, public posturing, and denial, this is crucially important. The addictive culture and the addictive church maintain themselves by non-confrontationally lying and covering up. They are obsessed with control and will do anything to keep it.

During the 1970s I served on a national Presbyterian task force that studied the ordination of "self-affirming, practicing homosexual persons." After our committee had been meeting for a short time, it became clear to me that it was a setup. After expending a substantial amount of time and money, some felt that the outcome had been determined before the first meeting. The chairperson and a majority of committee members had been carefully chosen to represent the view of the church administration: gays should be ordained. A token minority made things look fair. Consultations were held with people of varying opinions across the country so that the Church at large would be given the illusion that the process was open. Experts, such as sex researcher Dr. William Masters of Masters and Johnson, gave the study scientific credibility. In reality, the process remained a setup. Even the person who composed the majority report had been prechosen (much to the dismay of some in the majority who wanted to be in on the writing).

Later I related my experiences to the then president of the Covenant Church. He assured me that as president he too used his executive privilege to stack the deck. He counseled me to "include just enough opposition to defuse conflict in order to appear fair. They can ventilate without having real power." Using these tactics, Church leadership keeps us confused, powerless, and controlled. They appear to do one thing while doing exactly the opposite. This is addictive behavior. Surrounded by lies, who will tell us the truth? Jesus will.

It is out of Jesus' self-giving that he warned people about pretentious piety, raving lust, unforgiven anger, materialistic obsession, and satanic deception. What possible personal benefit could he have received from such cutting remarks? What popular preacher would tell us that it's harder for a camel to pass through the eye of a needle than for a rich man to enter the

kingdom of God? What was there to gain by summoning people to take up their crosses and follow him to death? What
advantage did he receive from warning against praying long
prayers and exhorting people to wash their faces and smile
when they fasted? What was in it for Jesus when he offended
intellectuals by commending people to become as little children in order to expose their hearts? There was no apparent
advantage to Jesus in any of these positions except a clear conscience. No, there was something deeper. He told the truth for
others' advantage rather than for his advantage. Today, what he
receives from the Father, he delivers to us. We're on his heart
and he wants us to be people of the truth.

As we begin to relate to Jesus, who is the truth, we will start
telling the truth ourselves. We won't be able to use secrecy and
deception in order to maintain control. I know of a well-known
evangelical leader who recently fired his divorced organist.
Rather than approaching him privately with love and concern,
he gave him the news through the Sunday morning announce-
ments. I know a church that stated publicly that an assistant
pastor resigned in order to go back to graduate school. In truth,
he was really fired for low performance. I even have a friend
who was asked by a burned out pastor to preach one Sunday.
Without warning, the pastor then announced to the congregation before his sermon that my friend would immediately be
taking over the church. All of these examples show us the
addictive church in action. The church uses secrecy and deception in order to maintain control. Unfortunately, it usually
works.

As we begin to relate to Jesus, who is the truth, we will no
longer be able to cover our selfishness with lies or manipulate
people by our distortions. We will no longer be able to protect
ourselves behind false fronts, masking our fear of exposure by
deceit. Out of my fear of other people's anger and rejection,
I've often waffled with the truth. As Jesus continually heals me,
however, I am becoming free to be myself and to know what

I think. I am free to know what I want to say and let the chips fall where they may. It's beginning to feel good! This is the work of the self-giving Jesus in me.

The Self-Giving Jesus Releases His Power

Along with loving us and telling us the truth, Jesus shows us his self-giving nature by releasing his power. After Jesus was anointed by the Spirit of God during his baptism, he was thrust out into the wilderness to do battle with the devil. After his victory there, the Spirit filled him again, launching him on his public ministry. In Luke 4:18–21, Jesus confirmed this work of the Spirit when he read from the Isaiah scroll in the synagogue at Nazareth:

> The Spirit of the Lord is upon Me,
> Because He anointed Me to preach the gospel to the poor.
> He has sent Me to proclaim release to the captives,
> And recovery of sight to the blind,
> To set free those who are downtrodden,
> To proclaim the favorable year of the Lord.

Continuing, he commented, "Today, this Scripture has been fulfilled in your hearing." By this proclamation he made it clear that he didn't come to form a new religion or even run a reform movement. Instead he responded to God's revelation and the Spirit's promptings to go to the poor, the sick, and the oppressed. He would go on to meet human needs wherever he found them. Since the Spirit was continuously in him, the sick would merely touch him and find healing. As he was touched, he would feel a surge of power going out to transform others. No wonder people pressed in to be near Jesus. As Francis Mac-Nutt once said to me, "If you want to start a worldwide movement, just heal a few people." Jesus did both through the power of the Spirit.

When Jesus spoke, the blind saw and the lame walked. He was like a doctor; his patientload included much of Israel. He came, not for the well, but for the sick. While he healed by the power of the Holy Spirit, it wasn't without personal cost to himself. When Jesus came to earth, he renounced heaven's glory and confined himself to the limitations of human flesh. He was left alone to become tired and harassed by the multitudes. He made himself vulnerable to the stink and stench of our fallen race. It's Jesus who now carries our sorrows in his heart as he extends his hand to pull us from the fire. It was Jesus who finally bore our sins in his own body on the tree.

Power and sacrifice, power and suffering, power and self-giving—this was authentic New Testament Christianity. It was with this knowledge that Jesus said to his disciples, "In the world you have tribulation, but take courage, I have overcome the world" (John 16:33). Paul echoed this truth when he told the Romans "we also exult in our tribulations" and reminded the Thessalonians "you also became imitators of us and of the Lord, having received the word in much tribulation with the joy of the Holy Spirit." It is the self-giving Jesus who promises to minister his power through us, but, like him, it will cost us everything.

In the history of the Church, revival has always been sparked by the coming of the Spirit in power. While this is a familiar picture to the Pentecostal and Charismatic movements, it was really the heartbeat of historic Christianity long before this century. John Wesley wrote of his experience in an entry dated January 1, 1739:

> Mr. Hall, Hinching, Ingham, Whitefield, Hutching and my brother Charles were present at our love feast in Fetter Lane with about sixty of our brethren. About three in the morning as we were continuing instant in prayer the power of God came mightily upon us, insomuch that many cried out for exulting joy and many fell to the ground. As soon as we

were recovered a little from the awe and amazement at the presence of His Majesty, we broke out with one voice, "We praise Thee O God, we acknowledge Thee to the Lord."[2]

It was men like John Wesley who were used to explode the Evangelical Awakening in England and the American colonies.

The famous nineteenth-century American evangelist, Dwight L. Moody, had a similar Spirit encounter. While raising funds to build a new church in Chicago after a fire had destroyed the city, he found that he hungered for the filling of the Holy Spirit. He recalled:

> My heart was not in the work of begging . . . I could not appeal. I was crying all the time that God would fill me with His Spirit. Well, one day, in the city of New York—oh, what a day!—I cannot describe it, I seldom refer to it; it is almost too sacred an experience to name. Paul had an experience of which he never spoke for fourteen years. I can only say that God revealed Himself to me, and I had such an experience of His love that I had to ask Him to stay His hand. I went to preaching again. The sermons were not different; I did not present new truths, and yet hundreds were converted. I would not now be placed back where I was before that blessed experience if you should give me all the world—it would be as the small dust of the balance.[3]

Here was a man who was changed by the self-giving Jesus, who released his love and power in him. His ministry would never be the same.

What was true for past generations is true for the Church today. Such a release of the power of the Spirit will recover the life of the Church as was seen in the Book of Acts. We will see fervent evangelism, healing and deliverance, bold intercession, and a hunger for apostolic teaching. The Church will be a transparent community filled with an awesome sense of the holy love of God in our midst.

The Self-Giving Jesus Invests in Us

Jesus not only gives us his love, truth, and power, but also invests his life in us and for us. By forming an inner group of apostles, Jesus symbolically reconstituted the twelve tribes of Israel. This, however, wasn't a mere symbolic act; Jesus called them to be with him. This meant intimate communion. Like a rabbi who trained his pupils by what he said and did, so Jesus let himself be known to his men. They saw him eat. They watched him sleep. They heard him pray. After they observed his teaching, they peppered him with questions in private. They were able to hear explanations of his public discourses. Through all their observations he was training them to be extensions of himself in the world. He gave them his word and showed them his works, expecting them to speak and do the same. He taught them to preach the kingdom of God, heal the sick, and cast out demons. He was the living model of what he expected them to be. They learned by being in intimate communion with him. It is no wonder they ended up turning the world upside down after the Holy Spirit descended on them. The apostles became more and more functional as they related to the functional Jesus. He not only invested himself in them, but also invested himself for them—which ended up costing him everything.

Jesus completely fulfilled his self-giving nature by going to the cross. Gold jewelry and church altars have blunted the harshness of his death. We no longer hear the crunch of bones and the painful cries. We no longer smell the stench of blood. We no longer see the deformed bodies, and watch life drain away. Jesus was God's perfect sacrifice, bleeding like a slain lamb, bearing both taunts and transgressions. He knew that all authority has been given into his hands, but he washed feet and, on the cross, washed our sins. Here, indeed, was the one fully self-giving person, the likes of which the world had never known.

Jesus wasn't an all-consuming addict; he was a receiver. He received the Father's presence in times of intimate communion. He received the Father's purpose during revelation that gave direction to his mission. He received the Spirit with anointing power. Out of his security, he also received the love and affection of people, without pushing them away because of their unworthiness, in order to retain his own authority and prideful independence.

Jesus was and is a giver. He returns the love of the Father, and then gives us the Father's presence and purpose. As the God-Man, Jesus brings the Father to us, and restores our fallen humanity. We not only learn to live fearlessly and freely, but also selflessly. As the one truly functional person, he alone can heal our addictions and codependency. He alone can tear off our masks and expose the fear and shame that lie underneath without destroying us. He alone can heal our being wound, securing us to the God who has made us for himself, and take us to his heart forever.

Part Three

Becoming a Functional Person

· · ·

Chapter 8

Giving Up Fear

.   .   .

The Christian life is one of crisis and process. After the crisis of conversion, we live the rest of our lives in the process of growing in Christ. After the crisis of recognizing addictive behavior, we live in the process of withdrawal and refocusing ourselves on loving God. The processes will be punctuated by further crises as we continue along the way of discipleship. These crises will be brought about by new invasions of God's Spirit and potential relapses back into or further detachments from our addictions. Throughout the journey, the goal will remain clear. It is God's intention to repopulate the planet with representations of himself. How exactly, though, does he make this happen?

Many answers have been given to the above question. Bookstores are filled with manuals on discipleship. Every church and Christian organization has its special approach to reproducing Christ's life in the believer. Much of this material centers on building the believers' faith, filling their heads with biblical truths, and leading them into a life of obedience, all of which are important. Unfortunately, however, discipleship isn't a program but a relationship that flows from the Father's unconditional love through his Son. This relationship must always center on relating to Jesus, the only fully functional person, and then relating to each other in a community in the process of becoming healthy. Only then can the Christian community be the true Church. Rather than being sterile and burdensome, the disciplines of the Christian life will make sense and become liberating.

We can only fully become Jesus' disciples if we allow him to probe the depths of our being. He must expose our personal, generational, and environmental sins, while forgiving and healing us. Otherwise, we will go through life carrying excess baggage from the past and inflicting that pain on others. True discipleship must be built on releasing the false self and its attachments, shedding the fear and shame that binds us, and becoming free from the poisonous pedagogy of our dysfunctional families that compound our addictions and codependency. As a result, we will become "holy"—the whole people God created us to be—set apart to be like him and to obey him in this world.

The New Testament contains substantial teachings, exhortations, corrections, and examples of mutual ministry. We can't allow discipleship, though, to become formless piety. How can we find an effective road to healing that embraces a biblical model but isn't legalistic? A time-honored answer comes from the Twelve-Step program of Alcoholics Anonymous (A.A.).

It's important to know that these simple A.A. directives were originally written with a specific Christian content. A.A. has its roots in the Oxford Group Movement whose founder, the Reverend Frank Buchman, was converted at the Keswick Convention in England in 1908. As a renewal movement within existing churches, the Oxford Group stressed new birth through a conviction of sin, complete surrender to the will of God, confession of sins to one or more other persons, and making restitution for wrongs whenever possible. A believer could only remain a "true Christian" by changing others.[1] No wonder that when A.A. was first conceived, Jesus was the Higher Power who alone could set the alcoholic free. The specific reference to Jesus was dropped as more and more people gravitated to the program. Because A.A. was conceived in Christ, the concepts refocused in Christ can be both biblical and healing.

The A.A. philosophy is centered in a step-by-step process known as the Twelve Steps. The purpose behind the Twelve Steps is to help alcoholics surrender to God. After this surrender, they are held accountable for their lives. The weakness of the Twelve Steps is their implied moralism and the oversimplification of personal responsibility. Since the Christian life is a relationship and not just rules for living, these steps can only help addicts grow in that relationship. If addicts focus only on responsibility for their own lives, they may fail to see the other side of the coin—abuse and generational and environmental sin have played a part in their addictions. They not only need to make restitution to those they have hurt, but also must forgive themselves and those who have hurt them. It's only through forgiveness that they will enjoy lasting freedom. Otherwise, they will continue to be angry people who miss the center of the Gospel: God's mercy through the cross. With these precautions in mind, the Twelve Steps have great value in aiding recovery from addictions and codependency.

The first three steps focus on the crisis of commitment. Let's take a fresh look at these steps.

Step One

"We admitted we were powerless over alcohol—that our lives had become unmanageable."[2] According to the "Big Book," the original guidebook of A. A., this is the first step to recovery. It painfully confesses that addictions, whether to substances, processes, or relationships, are no longer working and that we have to release them. We have been pretending that we are in control, but in actuality, we are out of control. Our freedom is bogus. I have a psychologist friend who said, "When I became a Christian, I had to give up my illusion of control." Addicts must make a similar surrender, involving indescribable suffering and agony.

Giving up the illusion of control means abandoning the last defenses of our independent egos. It means renouncing the self-idolatry that goes all the way back to Eden. It means that false selves are now exposed for what they are. Since destruction precedes reconstruction, these false selves must die. After Jesus has confronted us, provoking our crises of surrender, we will be forced to give up our addictive attachments. Gerald May points out that we don't lose the objects of our attachments so much as lose the attachments themselves.[3] In other words, we lose the strength of our addictive behavior that made gods out of these objects. Realizing that we must get rid of these makes us feel fearful, courageous, and grace-filled all in the same moment. Perhaps the biggest fear is that when we admit our powerlessness, there will be nothing left but holes in our souls. At this frightening possibility, we must remember that we are only at Step One. God wants to use these moments to come into our lives and fill us.

This admission of impotence only comes through crisis. The crises of admitting that we are powerless over our lives comes as we hit bottom—sometimes with a bounce, sometimes with a crash. For alcoholics this may be a gathering of intimate friends who show up on cue and confront them with the facts of their behavior and its consequences, commonly referred to as planned intervention. Caught in this loving crunch, they often break through denial. Through this intervention, fear is exposed and change becomes possible. Other crises may arise from less staged events. They may include the death of a loved one, the loss of a job, the end of a relationship, a divorce, a physical illness, or upheaval in the Church. A crisis may come at conversion when God simply stops us in our tracks like he did Paul on the Damascus Road.

Remember, the crisis of impotency is truly biblical. It was pride that separated humanity from God in Eden. It was pride that attracted humans to the bogus promise that they could become like their idea of a controlling God. It was pride that led us to abandon him and attach ourselves to the objects of our addictions. It's only when this pride is broken that healing can begin. The Bible says that God resists the proud but gives grace to the humble. It promises that he will have a day of judgment against all arrogance. It was with human pride in mind that Jesus said that all must become as little children in order to enter the kingdom of God. The admission of our own powerlessness prepares us to receive God's power. The admission that our lives are unmanageable prepares us for God's management. Giving up control will begin to remove the gnawing fear inside.

God will break the hard hearts of the self-righteously religious who come to Step One. He will strip "elder brothers" of performances, righteous works, presumptions, judgments, and secret rage. As those elder brothers, we will give up the law and the spiritual pride that goes with it. Where will that leave us? We will be on our faces, mumbling that we are powerless and that our lives, yes, even our religious lives, have become unmanageable. We will be on our faces, admitting that our codependent service to the church, our workaholism, and our continual rescue of others, hide the emptiness inside. We will be on our faces admitting that our attachments to money, food, sex, relationships, and our own self-images are idolatrous. This is the first step on the path of healing, and we must take it with guts and God's grace.

I have admitted my own powerlessness more than once. My first crisis was during my conversion. I realized how much Jesus loved me and how I shared responsibility for his death. My heart was broken; I knew in that moment that I could no longer manage my own life. Another crisis came when my wife Kathryn and I, in deep emotional pain, admitted that we were powerless over our relationship. Years later, I was broken once again when I was fired as a pastor. I then knew that I was powerless over the Church. I became separated from my "drug of choice" and all of my codependent relationships. Numb, depressed, and empty, I retreated into myself. All my plans, hopes, and dreams lay shattered at my feet. This was God's severe mercy and my first step to healing. All of us will go through this crisis more than once as God brings down our idols, setting us free to love him. Acknowledging that we are out of control is the first step to becoming like the fearless Jesus.

Step Two

"[We] came to believe that a Power greater than ourselves could restore us to sanity."[4] Step Two seems to imply that our addictions and codependencies have made us insane. If this is the case, an addict has a choice—life or death. For the alcoholic or drug addict this choice becomes very real in a physical sense. Many of my addict friends only saw their insanity by courting death through overdosing. The danger of our religious addictions and codependencies is that they perpetuate the illusion of life while being just as deadly. We can't see this until the veil is lifted from our eyes.

The second step opens with the statement "[we] came to believe." Belief, then, is the issue after admission. We can give in to faith or despair. Once our denial is overcome and we see our false selves, with all our addictions and our fears, we will either die (quickly or slowly) or seek help beyond ourselves.

Where can we find such help? We must look beyond this world. We have to see that apart from Jesus, everyone else is as insane as we are; the asylum is being run by the inmates. Everyone is an addict, suffering from personal, environmental, and generational sin. Everyone masks shame behind proper costumes and false selves. Why should we entrust our lives to this world and its ideologies? Can the blind lead the blind? Clearly, we need a "Power greater than ourselves" that this world can't provide. We need a Power greater than any self-help group. We don't need another codependent rescuer. This Power can't be another addiction in the form of drugs, relationships, or church. This Power can be found in God alone, the only one who has never abandoned us, however lost or lonely we have felt. God doesn't want to be another addiction, however. As Gerald May says, God will not allow himself to become another object of our attachment "because . . . [God] desires full love, not addiction."[5]

The God of the Bible dwells in light unapproachable. He is the sovereign Lord who created the world from his throne. He is the awesome judge who holds us accountable for our lives. He is also the loving Lord who sent his Son to redeem us from our fallen state.

Jesus, who has conquered Satan, sin, and death now reigns over the universe in a position of authority at God's right hand. One day God will consummate all things in Christ's glorious return. This is the, "Power greater than ourselves." This Power is no abstraction; this Power is a person we can trust. That person is the Lord Jesus Christ, who brings eternal, unconditional love from God's heart to ours. Our relationship with God is restored. The sense of abandonment is gone. For this reason, we cry out, "Abba! Father!" When we open up our hearts to this personal Power, Jesus invades our lives through the Holy Spirit. As my friend Jerry Moser puts it, "God wants to zip us open and jump inside."

The living God is the Power that will restore us to sanity. The only question is whether we will believe this. If we get stuck at this point, we need to pray, "O God, give me the faith to believe that through Jesus you are the Power greater than myself and that you alone can heal me." God will answer this prayer as we keep praying from our surrendered, unmanageable hearts. We will begin to sense that Jesus is here for us. Faith will begin to replace fear. This is the next step in becoming like the fearless Jesus.

Step Three

"[We] made a decision to turn our will and our lives over to the care of God as we understood Him."[6] This statement is vague at best. This God is often described today as a Higher Power. Such vague terminology could lead people to make anything a higher power—an A.A. group, any type of religious experience, a therapist, a pastor, a guru, or even a new addiction. Addictive relationships can easily form with an A.A. sponsor or a church leader. Originally, in A.A., the third step encouraged a clear surrender to Jesus. He is Lord and Savior, not as we understand him, but as he understands himself. As we're confronted by him, we're called into account for our lives. He is King. Will we submit to him? He is Lord. Will we serve him? He is Savior. Will we receive him? If we recognize that we're not God, we must meet Jesus on his terms rather than on our own. A more appropriate Step Three would be: "We made a decision to turn our will and our lives over to the care of God, as He is revealed in His Son, the Lord, Jesus Christ."

The third step calls for the surrender of our wills. It doesn't mean Jesus wants to break our wills so we can be filled with poisonous pedagogy. Jesus doesn't beat us until we give up. On the contrary, he took the punishment that we deserve. Out of his undying love, he woos us to himself. As Jesus humbles himself before us and washes our feet, he breaks our pride. Through his acts of mercy, he crushes our hard hearts and fills them with his love and compassion. Once this happens, at the very core of our being, our abandoned shame base starts to heal. The God we rejected through endless acts of rebellion forgives us and comes into our hearts. Here is a miracle. We are born again.

On a psychological level, as we give our desires to Christ, we detach ourselves from our addictions. This means repenting of idols, stopping addictive behaviors, and going through the stress of withdrawal. Only then will we be set free to love

God and our neighbors as ourselves. I must confess that as a Church addict, becoming detached requires a lot of grace. At times God has had to separate me physically from the Church —once when I resigned and once when I was fired. At other times, he has worked on me through the Spirit by wedding my heart to himself in new ways, freeing me to love him once again. Whatever the means, we must be separated from our addictive attachment to the Church so we can really love and care for the Christian community in freedom rather than with compulsion.

According to Step Three, Jesus receives our wills and our lives. This means that we offer him souls that he claims for his kingdom and renews by his Spirit. We are in for total renovation.

At this point, Jesus will begin to deal with our addictive attachments one by one. As Gerald May writes:

> The same processes that are responsible for addiction to alcohol and narcotics are also responsible for addiction to ideas, work, relationships, power, moods, fantasies, and an endless variety of other things. We are all addicts in every sense of the word. . . . Addiction also makes idolators of us all, because it forces us to worship these objects of attachment, thereby preventing us from truly, freely loving God and one another. Addiction breeds willfulness within us, yet, again paradoxically, it erodes our free will and eats away at our dignity. Addiction, then, is at once an inherent part of our nature and an antagonist of our nature. It is the absolute enemy of human freedom, the antipathy of love.[7]

As the attachment to our addictions is broken, we will be free to deal healthily with the things that have bound us, including the Church.

If Jesus offers us such tremendous freedom, what would keep us from the surrender called for in Step Three?

First, we may fear that if we give our lives to Jesus, we're really giving them up to an abuser. I know many people who believe that if they surrender themselves to Jesus, they will be punished or forced to be a missionary in a remote part of the world. They think that if they come home drunk, Jesus will be angry. Some are haunted by dark pictures of Jesus as a vengeful and vindictive Christ. They are often wounded by abusive parochial or Sunday school teachers who represented Jesus in this way out of their own fear and anger. Others have a guilt-centered relationship with him because they only know the Jesus who was crucified by their sins. They have never experienced the risen Jesus who was crucified for their sins and forgives and delivers them from the wrath to come.

What we must see is that the Father that Jesus reveals loves us unconditionally. God takes total responsibility for our lives. If we have unresolved childhood abuses, he will heal the pain. Why would he inflict more abuse on us? As we face abuse issues head-on, praying over them, restorations will begin. To surrender to anything or anyone less than Jesus, is to surrender to another addictive idol. This will only keep us in bondage. To our horror, we will find that we have simply exchanged one tyrant for another, giving ourselves up to be abused again. To surrender to Jesus, however, is to fall into the arms of the living God. Like the prodigal son, we come home to the Father's house and find a party prepared for us.

Second, we may resist the call to surrender because we're unwilling to go through the withdrawals. Separating ourselves from addictive attachments can result in stress, depression, and disorientation. Although we should realistically be prepared for these circumstances, there will be times when God comes with such powerful deliverance, that all we will feel is incredible joy. I have a close friend who was addicted to heroin for several years. One night, when he was desperate for a fix, his sister confronted him with the Gospel. He not only received Jesus on the spot but also was filled with the Holy Spirit. From that moment, he was healed from his addiction. He didn't have to go through the withdrawals that he had suffered from when he had tried to stop before. We must remember, even in a case like this, that the devil is the active enemy who contests each work of God, bringing doubt, confusion, and the desire to use again.

Beyond Intervention

The first three steps provoke crises. We take the first step by admitting that we are powerless over our life and that it is unmanageable. We then come to believe that we need an outside Power to heal our insanity. This "Higher Power" is the real Lord, Jesus Christ, not the Sunday school Jesus, not the stained-glass Jesus, but the eternal Son of God, the only fully functional person. With fear and trembling, we must now detach from our addictions and give our desire (attachment) and our wills over to him.

While our healing begins in crisis, it must also become a part of our process. We must daily admit that we are powerless. We must daily believe that only God can keep us sane. We must daily give God our wills and our lives. We must daily find our center in Jesus. They say in A.A. that people must turn it over daily (or hourly, or minute by minute). Once we have made this initial commitment—once Jesus has our deeds, our car keys, our American Express cards, our address books, our hunger, our partying, our families, our self-image, our churches, our ministries, our leaders, our budgets, and our codependent relationships—we are ready to go on to the next step. As we're delivered from our addictions, we're delivered from our fears. We can, then, begin to mirror the fearless Jesus. He has placed us on the road to freedom.

Chapter 9

Getting Free

•　　　•　　　•

After we admit that we are powerless over our lives and turn them over to our Higher Power, Jesus, the fear behind our false selves will be exposed. As this fear is acknowledged, Jesus comes to comfort and heal us from the shame that lies at the base of our lives. We can begin to experience his freedom more and more as we live with him. How do we take practical steps to help this come about? Steps Four through Seven show us the way.

Step Four

"[We] made a searching and fearless moral inventory of ourselves."[1] Jesus comes to free us from the past. This includes our bondage to Satan, this fallen world system (including family control, religious legalism, and economic fear), sin, the law, and the flesh (our false front that masks our deep shame inside). As we make our "searching and fearless moral inventory," much of this will be specifically exposed. It will include the hurts that we've inflicted on others as well as the hurts that have been inflicted upon us.

To begin a moral inventory, we need to block out substantial time by ourselves. We need to quiet our hearts and meditate. As we reflect over our past, we must first face family relationships honestly and squarely. Were our families dysfunctional? How did we develop within them? What roles did we play? Did we grow or merely survive? We must go back to our childhood and ask God to break through any denial or rationalization that we may have created about the past. If there is a significant memory lapse regarding childhood, we're probably blocking untreated pain and abuse. Professional therapists, pastoral counselors, or mature Christian friends can help us recover those lost years. Like the fourth step states, our inventory must be "searching." We must pray for the grace to shine the light of truth on every dark spot.

While we should strive for honesty, we must also guard against perfectionism that will demand we uncover and uproot absolutely everything all at once. Grace covers all our sins and all the abuse we have ever received. Nevertheless, we still need to be aware of our key personal and moral issues. We want to expose the blocks that keep us wounded. We pray, "Lord, help me to remember what I need to know now. Bring other things to my mind that you want me to deal with in your time."

Our inventory must also be "fearless." Nothing must hold us back from trying to see things as they really are; only the fearless Jesus can give us the grace to do so.

The fourth step will expose the perversion of our thoughts as well as our actions. We must courageously face the damage we've done to our parents and family out of anger and rebellion. Our inventory will include all the people that we've used, abused, and rejected, including our sexual sins, exploits, conquests, and adulteries.

We need to catalog the idols and false gods of false religions that have seduced us. Our inventories may include any contact with the occult, even encounters with seemingly innocent things like palm readings, astrologers, or ouji boards. They may also include any participation in Satanism, Mormonism, Jehovah Witnesses, Buddhism, ESP, transcendental medication, or various New Age religions. All these kinds of spirituality are seductive and morally wrong. These practices have been the means of humanity's rebellion against the one living God—a God who insists that we have no other gods before Him.

Our inventories need to look at addictive issues. What were our parents' addictions? In what ways were they role models for our own addictions? How have we willfully (and compulsively) participated in addictive substances, processes, and relationships? How have we used alcohol and drugs? How have we used exercise and food?

What have we done with people? We need to examine our close friendships. We must look at our sexual history. We have to remember who we went to school with, lived next to, worked with, socialized with, and dated. How have we handled even casual encounters? Who have we cheated and used? How have we contributed to the addictive culture in which we live? How have we contributed to the addictive church that we've served? Have we participated in its perfectionism, judgmentalism, and fear-driven obsessive control? How have we manipulated others and people pleased? We need to spell all of this out clearly. It's true that we've been compulsively hooked by many addictions; it's also true that we've willfully participated in those addictions by harboring the idolatrous assumption that we can control and manage them. We've promised again and again that we will quit tomorrow, but we need to admit that the facades of control have made us insane.

Next, we need to examine our false selves. What have we used to deceive people? How have we hidden our true selves? What images have we fostered? What deceptions have we played out? What are the fears that have driven us? Of what have we been ashamed?

While we should make a "searching and fearless moral inventory of ourselves," we need to understand how others have hurt us in order to be totally healed. As we survey our past relationships, we will find that we have not only sinned against people, but they have also sinned against us. While I freely admit rebelling against my parents, I also need to admit the abusive use of poisonous pedagogy. Many of us need to be healed of pain that has been inflicted on us. Addictive behaviors often go back generations. I've inherited some of my addictions and codependencies from my family. If a parent is an alcoholic, then the child is a codependent and that is that. My friend's father is a workaholic and an alcoholic. He is also a Christian and an elder in his church. His son became an alcoholic and a sex addict. When my friend finally received treatment, he discovered that he had carried on the generational abuse that he had received from his father. Through the father and the son's recovery, the generational, addictive chain was broken.

Beyond family relationships, I have to also deal with friends, classmates, coaches, teachers, employers, Christians, Sunday school teachers, pastors and lay leaders who have rejected me, judged me, manipulated me, abused me, deceived me, and kept me in fear.

Step Five

"[We] admitted to God, to ourselves, and to another human being the exact nature of our wrongs [and the wrongs committed against us]."[2] Making moral inventories leads us to the crucial step of confession, setting us free from guilt and bondage in order to be like the free Jesus. We must confess our wrongs to God because they are violations against his moral will. He created us and, therefore, knows what is best for us. He has the right to order our lives. (His desires will be fulfilled on earth, as they are in heaven.) When we exhibit self-righteousness, pride, greed, and anger, when we lie, steal, or indulge in sexual sin, when we make attachments to substances, processes, and people, we are not only hurting ourselves and other people, but also violating God himself. In essence, we're not acknowledging God as God. We're not loving him freely. We are rejecting his plan and purpose for creation. When we admit to God "the

exact nature of our wrongs," however, we're agreeing that we have sinned against, or violated, God's moral will.

Confession is the only way we can be free from captivity. Through confession, we're not only admitting our sins, but also giving ourselves to God to be brought into a right relationship with him through the death of his Son. We're asking him to send a wave of cleansing grace through our hearts. Through confession, God not only sets us free from the past, but also frees us for the future—a future filled with the adventure of living with and serving him in this world.

It's incredible how many of us live with unconfessed sin. We limp through life carrying a load of guilt, while hiding it behind our false selves. This only perpetuates dishonesty, spiritual pride, and deep inner loneliness. No one really knows us. A congregational confession of sin on Sunday sedates our pain momentarily, but hardly lifts the load. We must truly confess a step at a time, bringing our moral inventory to the Lord in prayer.

The New Testament tells us to confess our sins to one another as well as to God. James 5:16 says that if a person is sick he should call the elders to have them anoint him with oil and pray over him. Any sins that he had committed would be forgiven. (If there was a link between sicknesses and sins, that would be broken.) James 5:16 concludes, "Therefore, confess your sins to one another, and pray for one another, so that you may be healed. The effective prayer of a righteous man [or woman] can accomplish much." Now, through confession, we are detaching from that which has held us captive in our hearts. This is the only way to make the break from our entanglements and turn again to loving God with all that we are.

Here is a sample prayer: "In Jesus' name I confess _____ as sin and ask you, heavenly Father, to forgive me and to cleanse me with the blood of your Son." As we admit our wrongs to God we are admitting them to ourselves at the same time. But we cannot stop here.

To carry our confession to completion, we need to find one or two nonjudgmental, mature, Christian friends who will be elders for us. They need to be people who have experienced the forgiveness and healing of God. They need to maintain confidentiality after they have prayed with us over our inventories. Together, each item in the inventories will be addressed and released.

This idea of admitting "to another human being the exact nature of our wrongs," may seem offensive. Some Protestants might think that this is too reminiscent of the Roman Catholic practice of going to the confessional rather than going directly to Jesus. The real reason we probably balk at confession is that it's embarrassing and humiliating to let other people hear the secrets of our hearts. How could we let others see our darkness? Besides, if we let other people know our shame, won't they use it against us?

If we don't seek others out in confession, we will miss an important spiritual, relational, and biblical truth—God ministers to us through others. They are often the means through which Jesus makes his intercession and mercy effective. As we confess, our hypocrisy will blessedly melt. We will no longer be religious but real. After people see our brokenness and tears they will extend their love and mercy in Jesus' name. Confessing to other believers shields us from excessively spiritualizing our current trials and temptations. I remember a few years ago, I became obsessed thinking about a particular sexual fantasy. It plagued me and held me captive. Finally, I revealed it to a trusted brother who heard my pain and prayed for me. In that moment the fantasy's power was broken, never to return.

Our chosen elders should give us Scriptural assurances like 1 John 1:9: "If we confess our sins, He is faithful and righteous to forgive us our sins and to cleanse us from all unrighteousness." We need people to remind us that God hears and answers us again and again. As Luther said, we are so thick headed that we need to have the Gospel continually pounded into us. We also need our brothers and sisters to pray that God will make his cleansing real to us in Jesus' name.

When the Bible tells us to confess our sins to one another, it's not leading us to an anonymous priest. This would be like confessing to a Christian who isn't capable of making a similar confession. We should be careful, then, that we don't become vulnerable to self-righteous people who dump criticism and condemnation on us in the form of good advice. Jesus' word to the woman taken in adultery is to be our word to each other, ". . . neither do I condemn you, go and sin no more" (John 8:11). The friend who heard my confession came to me sometime later to reveal a deep sickness and shame that was enslaving him. He could trust me because I had trusted him. As he shared his sorrow with me, the healing began.

Self-disclosure breeds intimacy. Trusted brothers or sisters who hear our confessions will also keep us accountable. In my experience, if I confess my sins to God in the presence of a forgiving and broken fellow Christian, I'm not only strengthened by the act but also drawn closer to the brother who hears my confession.

God has forgiven us, so we must forgive those who have wronged us. Our prayer on Sunday, "Forgive us our debts, as we forgive our debtors . . ." (Matt. 6:12), must not mock us the rest of the week. For example, if we were abused as a children by alcoholic or workaholic parents, we need to forgive them. If we hold on to the anger that was caused by our pain, we will continue to live in states of unforgiveness. This only hurts us. We must believe and act on the Gospel of the cross, which means forgiveness and freedom. As we forgive our abusers, we will no longer be controlled by our anger toward them. Our initial responses to former attacks won't push us around any longer. As we deal honestly with our emotions, we will be free at last from all dimensions of abuse.

Once we have forgiven our childhood abusers, we're ready to grieve our losses. The grieving process includes breaking through denial and releasing anger and sorrow. If we try to avoid this process, we will continue to be emotional cripples. I can't stress enough how important this is. Alice Miller says, "It is [the] . . . lack of hope of ever being able to express repressed traumata by means of relevant feelings that most often causes severe psychological problems."[3] Unresolved childhood grief can leave our inner child in an emotionally stunted state. John Bradshaw says many people need help finishing "their unresolved grief from childhood—griefs resulting from abandonment, abuse in all forms, the neglect of childhood developmental dependency needs, and the enmeshments that result from family-system dysfunction."[4] For full healing to happen, we must ask God to help us experience our emotional pains before we can let them go. One friend told me of the horror of lying in bed and hearing his drunk father pull the belt out of his pants as he came toward the room to beat him. No wonder as an adult he had trouble sleeping alone. What now can he do? He needs to grieve this loss of his father's protection and love that he deserved as a child. He needs to weep over the irrational punishment that brought terror into his life. He also needs to admit his anger toward his dad, forgive him for his abuse, and forgive himself for harboring bitterness and resentment in his heart. This too will be a part of his healing. As he does this, similar abuse will not be passed on to his own children. The generational chain of sin will be broken. Moreover, he will not act out his abuse unconsciously in his relationships within the family of the Church. As he is set free, others will be set free as well.

My own inner child grief came when I realized how my dad's absence during World War II had wounded me. I pictured him, praying about his departure, and tried to imagine what it must have been like for him to leave me when I was four years old. I found myself weeping softly for him. Then I heard a little child's voice inside of me crying out, "Daddy, why did you have to go? I needed you so much." At the recognition of my own voice, fifty years of buried pain burst out; I began to be released from the abandonment and shame that I had felt. I prayerfully forgave my dad for unintentionally leaving me. I also had to forgive myself for carrying all these years of unconscious anger and fear. As a result of my fear of abandonment, rejection has been a major issue for me throughout most of my life. Because of my honest grieving, it is less of an issue now.

To be freed from fear is to be free to face our sins and acknowledge our pain before God and each other. Confession is not only "good for the soul," it is another step on the road to being free like Jesus. Christ alone can set us free from all our past bondages, enabling us to love God fully and our neighbors as ourselves.

Step Six

"[We] were entirely ready to have God remove all these defects of character."[5] It's one thing to confess our sins. It's another thing to want to be free from them and all the emotional hooks that leave us vulnerable to sin. For example, it's one thing to confess our lust. It's another thing to want to be free from consuming sexual passion and compulsive, pornographic fantasy. To be free, we must detach ourselves from sexual arousal that can become like a mood altering "drug." We must remove ourselves from the contexts that lead us to associate lust with dark behavior. We must give up using sexual passion to relieve depression and loneliness or release anger so we can channel our desire toward loving God instead.

After confession, we must answer Jesus' crucial questions to the lame man by the pool of Bethesda: Do we really want to be healed? If we answer yes, we're ready to move on to repentance from sin and all its benefits. Repentance simply means that we are ready for God to change us. This is not moralistic or legalistic. This move does not say we're ready to change ourselves, but rather, we're ready for God "to remove all these defects of character." It's by his grace and intervention alone that we will be set free.

Notice Step Six states we are "entirely ready" for God to demolish all that lies behind our false selves. This means that we have hit bottom and confessed our powerlessness in Step One. With disgust, we have seen through the deception of sin. Our moral failures and resulting addictions no longer work for us. Now, in despair over our lives, we cry out to God to change us.

Step Seven

"[We] humbly asked Him (God) to remove our shortcomings."[6] Step Seven goes beyond confession and asks God to change us. This starts with repentance and leads to detachment. In the Old Testament, "to repent" meant "to turn." When we repent, we turn from our sins. At the same time, we turn to God. We turn from self-will to his will. He is the only one worthy of our passion and desire. He is the only one worthy of our love and delight.

In Step Four we faced ourselves squarely. In Step Five we confessed our sins and received God's forgiveness.

Now our prayer will be to turn from these sins and, with God's grace, to not indulge in them again. If we are alcoholics, this means quitting drink. If we are codependents, this means not using other people.

Our turning must also include the supposed benefits of our sin. What is meant by benefits? If a person is having an affair, for example, the benefits could include companionship, excitement, sexual gratification, not having to deal honestly with a difficult marriage, and false comfort for a mid-life crisis. We need to renounce these benefits in Jesus' name.

We must also ask God to heal us from whatever abuses we received in the past that have contributed to our immoralities.

The sense of God's absence, generational sin, and poisonous pedagogy are all a part of the hole that we've tried to fill with our addictions. Along the way, we've lied and deceived others and ourselves. Now we're ready for God to change us. We ask him to remove our short comings, and heal our vulnerable points.

Our prayers may include, "Break my pride, make me humble. Break my addiction, make me free. Break my lying, make me honest." After our prayers of brokenness we must pray for God's Spirit to come and heal our being wounds. His presence will remove the abandonment shame base of our lives. God loves us. God accepts us. We are his. We are no longer worthless and alone, bouncing around in a meaningless universe. His Son has come for us and holds us in his strong grip.

We can now begin to pray for wholeness: "Jesus, make me fearless. Jesus, make me free." We can pray for God to fulfill his intention to repopulate the planet with images of himself. Jesus can make us as truly self-giving and functional as he is.

Chapter 10

Giving
Yourself Away

• • •

Why does God want us to give up our fears and be set free? He not only wants us to be fulfilled, but also wants us to be self-giving. God wants to make us into self-giving lovers like himself. Self-fulfillment is the by-product of loving like Jesus, not the goal of his work in us. How can we give ourselves away? Steps Eight through Twelve become our trustworthy guides. As we go through them, we must remember that the Christian life is occasionally crisis, but mostly process. It's a growth in grace as we continue to respond to God's work in us.

Step Eight

"[We] made a list of all persons we had harmed, and became willing to make amends to them all."[1] This leads us to become like the self-giving Jesus. Like our inventory in Step Four it requires reflection and prayer. We're asking God to expose the damage that we've done to others. An alcoholic might ask: Who have I stolen from in order to get money for booze? Who have I lied to about drinking? Who have I hurt by my emotional absence? Who have I abused when I binged? Who have I influenced toward alcoholism by my example?

It's more difficult to understand how we've harmed others if we've "helped" people through church addictions or codependent relationships. Since we are no longer in denial, we can begin to see how we have operated. A relational addict would ask: Who have I lied to out of fear? When have I not confronted someone with the truth? Who have I gossiped about in order to undermine his or her leadership? Who have I ministered to in order to get something for my benefit? How have I used people to make them give money? Who have I made feel guilty so that they will work for the church? How has my false flattery reinforced false selves? Who have I ministered to, because they were famous or important, in order to make me feel good? Who have I ministered to, because they were symbols of the oppressed, in order to give me ecclesiastical status or relieve my white upper-middleclass guilt? Who have I spent special time with or recruited into leadership because of their financial or social power in the community? How have I used the Church for my own needs and justified it as ministry? How have I played out the issues of my dysfunctional family in church family relationships?

As our lists of people grow, we must be "willing to make amends to them all." We need a lot of grace to do this. At this point, the self-giving Jesus will release his self-giving in us. We must see where we can use the truth against our own lies and deceptions. We must ask how we can recover what we've lost. Finally, we must be ready to act on our conclusions. Our attitude at this point is crucial. We need to join David in his prayer, "Create in me a clean heart, O God, And renew a steadfast spirit within me" (Ps. 51:10).

When we refuse to be dysfunctional and codependent within the Church any longer, people around us will be forced to face their own similar issues. Our healing will not be ours alone.

Through our journey together, the Church will begin to be the community Jesus intended it to be—a healing environment for us all, where love and truth abound. It is a hard road to free-dom and self-giving, but we must be willing to take it. We must be willing to die to ourselves to become more like Jesus.

Step Nine

"[We] made direct amends to such people wherever possible, except when to do so would injure them or others."[2] Now that we've made our moral inventories and lists of people we've harmed, it's time to implement behavioral change. We must be like Zaccheus, the chief tax collector of Jericho, who, when called by Jesus, gave half his goods to the poor and restored four times the amount to those he had defrauded. In the same way, alcoholics need to make amends to the people they've hurt by asking for forgiveness for all the pain they have caused. Honesty becomes the order of the day. Bad loans must be paid off and stolen money restored. At the same time, they may also have to forgive their alcoholic parents and any others who were role models for their addictions. Time and caring should now characterize their intimate relationships.

For those of us who are addicted to the Church, we may need to ask our spouses to forgive us for the long, lonely hours they spent while we were "serving the Lord." We may need to let our children know how wrong we were to break our prom-ises and miss their Little League games. We must tell church leaders how we've used them, manipulated them, and lied to them in order to maintain our codependencies and church addictions. Some of us may even have to tell our congregations how deceptive we've been, pretending we were "Preacher Perfect."

Breaking through this hypocrisy and deceit will create a moral and spiritual crisis. If we take Step Nine, however, we will be building barriers against the continuing ravages of our dis-eases. We will now be accountable to the Church. Our honesty will be a model to the addictive and codependent people around us. We can begin to free the Church from its sick accommodation to the addictive culture that keeps it so dysfunctional.

As we make amends to people, we must not act "when to do so would injure them or others." For example, if a pastor has begun to develop a special attachment to a woman who is not his wife, he needs to confess this to God and to another person; repent of the relationship; and renounce its supposed benefits. He also needs to ask God to heal him of the emotional hooks, avoid situations of intimacy, and restore fidelity to his marriage. At the same time, if this pastor admits his feelings to this woman and asks her forgiveness, he would most likely unnecessarily injure her and others. The confession might even create more intimacy between the pair. The confession of his sin to God and to his wife (depending on the security of their marriage) or to another person in confidence would be sufficient restoration. Any other amends would probably only be destructive or self-serving.

Making amends isn't easy. The proof of our freedom, however, is in our actions. We must not avoid this step because we fear hurting others. We're most likely afraid of being hurt ourselves by their responses. We must remember truth heals when it is spoken in love. We must pray that the self-giving Jesus will set us free to die to our false selves so that his true self can shine through us. We must pray for wisdom, so that we don't further damage people. We must never use these times of restoration to merely get rid of our guilt; after all, making amends is primarily for other people's good. Only after using this process with love for others, can we use it for our growth. A lot of excitement and surprises lie ahead when we move out in this step.

Step Ten

"[We] continued to take personal inventory and when we were wrong promptly admitted it."[3] As we know, the Christian life

is both crisis and process. Perfection is only found in Jesus. It's not surprising that healing from addiction and codependency is mostly a process. We will need God's continuing grace in order to detach ourselves from addictions again and again.

We need to stay in touch with ourselves and be aware of our vulnerability to relapses. If we frequently look over our motives, relationships, and behaviors, we will keep moving toward health. We must not become morose or excessively introspective. After all, we have already asserted that the Christian life is to be lived outside of ourselves. This self-giving move toward wholeness must come through brokenness, or we will become manipulative and self-serving. For this reason, we need to check ourselves by making continuous inventory. Through this method, we can promptly admit when we're wrong.

We need people around us who know our sickness and who will tell us when we're off course. Confession of sin, repentance of wrong-doing, and renunciation of the supposed benefits of sin will become thematic in our lives. The cross and the Lord's Supper will be central to the faith and experience of our new life in Christ. We will continue to live by the forgiveness of our sins offered us by the risen Lord. We will never be through needing his mercy and the benefits he pours out upon us.

Step Eleven

"[We] sought through prayer and meditation to improve our conscious contact with God as we understood Him, praying only for knowledge of His will for us and the power to carry that out."[4] Again, Christianity is not a religion but a relationship. Prayer is the means of its inauguration, maintenance, and growth. Through prayer we welcome Jesus into our lives and begin to walk with him day by day. Through prayer we grow in deeper intimacy with him, becoming more like him. Through

prayer we see God work through his power and ministry in our lives. This is the crucial means of improving our "conscious contact" with God.

Another important means is meditation. For us, this doesn't mean emptying our minds in an Eastern mystical fashion. Rather, it means filling our minds with the Word of God. As we wait upon the Lord to speak to us personally, we can test what we hear by the revelation in God's written Word. Through prayer and meditation we will develop what John Wimber calls a "secret history" with God. This history will grow by our going into the closet and praying to our Father. As we do this, God promises us a secret reward. As we open ourselves to God, He will disclose more and more of himself to us. As with our human families, we will build up memories of our time with God that will enrich our lives. As we grow in intimacy, our "Abba" relationship with him will deepen.

According to Step Eleven, we are to pray for two things: the knowledge of God's will and the power to live it out. In the traditional church we have concentrated on knowing and minimalized the power. We then wonder at our impotence. When Christianity exploded into the world, this was not the case. Jesus himself was empowered by the Holy Spirit at his baptism. He promised the same power to his disciples, which they received on the day of Pentecost. Again and again, the Book of Acts records empowering moments as the Gospel spreads. In 1 Corinthians 4:20, Paul wrote, "For the kingdom of God does not consist in words, but in power." This empowerment has been repeated throughout history in times of revival and missionary advances. In the church today, however, most of us know the presence of God but fear the power of God. In the context of our addictive culture, we need to maintain control. Rather than humbling our hearts and crying out to God to come in power and bring another Pentecost, our fears provide us an anemic church experience.

We live in a time, however, when God is releasing the power of the Spirit upon the Church again. Revival and renewal are in the air. A fresh wind is blowing. The closed universe of our scientific worldview is under siege. This should raise our expectations. But how can this movement become real to us?

First, we need to believe that the power of the Spirit is available today. Second, we need to repent of our known personal sin and pray for that power to come to us. If nothing happens immediately, we need to continue to pray. God is testing our intentions; he wants to know if we're serious and how we will use the power he gives us. Third, we need to find places where the power of God is operating, lay aside our shame, and ask people to pray for us. The work of the Spirit is infectious— caught, not just taught. We cannot manipulate God; God's power is his to give. Again, we must give up control and wait in faith for God to act.

Michael Cassidy, often called the "Billy Graham of Africa," recounts his experience of empowering during a renewal conference in South Africa. During a general session, the biblical text about a grain of wheat dying in order to bear much fruit hit Michael like a surgeon's knife. He recounts,

> Something deep and painful and crucifying and new was happening in me in those very moments. I could not restrain the tears. The grain of wheat which was my life had to die in new and deeper and truer ways if it was to bring forth fruit pleasing to God. . . . He wanted all of me. But the world, the flesh and the devil were still clutching. . . . It was painful to face. I had the Spirit, but did the Spirit have me?
>
> I don't know how long the struggle continued. Half an hour. Maybe more. During that time loving brothers and sisters cared for me and prayed with me.
>
> [That night] sleep would not come to me. Instead, quite out of the blue, the Spirit of praise came upon my soul. All

seemed to be release. All seemed to be freedom. Hour after hour I praised my God in unrestrained and unrestrainable doxology and song. In words of men and angels I rejoiced. No fatigue visited me that night. All my senses were vibrantly alive to God. The Holy Spirit was blessing me. Wave upon wave, it seemed. Flow upon flow. He seemed to be bubbling up from within, surrounding from without, ascending from below and descending from above!

Somewhere in the early hours of the morning I said to myself: "I don't know the correct biblical name for this, but this is the experience I've heard others talk of."[5]

Christianity is not a head trip. Only God's power will save us from religion, legalism, and hypocrisy. We have Jesus' word that if we who are evil know how to give good gifts to our children, how much more will our heavenly Father give the Holy Spirit to those who ask him.

If we can have intimacy with God, know how he wants us to live, and receive his strength to do so, then we can go for it! This is the way to a selfless life with Jesus.

Step Twelve

"Having had a spiritual awakening as the result of these steps, we tried to carry this message to alcoholics, and to practice these principles in all our affairs."[6] Has God really changed our lives? Are we free to give our selves away?

Finally, we can truthfully share the good news. We must give away the work God has done in us if we are to keep it. Otherwise, God's gifts become stale and stagnant, placing us in danger of relapsing into our old addictions. Simply stated, this step calls for evangelism. Our recovery is not merely for our own sakes; it is also for the sake of others. As we share the Twelve Steps, our healing continues. Self-giving becomes a lifestyle.

We must also "practice these principles in all our affairs" until they become part of the fabric of our lives. Consistency and maturity will be the results. This means that in everything we will admit our powerlessness, our inability to manage our lives, and our insanity without Jesus as our Higher Power. Every area of our lives—our own minds, wills, and emotions; our relationships, activities and possessions; our identity and destiny—will continually be detached from as we "turn our wills and our lives over to the care of God." Part of this process is the continuation of our "searching moral inventory." We will welcome confession, repentance, renunciation, accountability, and making amends.

While we follow the Twelve Step guidelines, we must remember that the changes taking place in us come from God's grace and Spirit alone. He will continue to remove our shortcomings. For this to happen, we need to get closer to him through prayer and meditation. We must ask for both knowledge of his will and the strength to live out that will. As we share our processes with others, they will become more and more our own. We will emerge from our addictions and codependencies with love and freedom to become part of the solution in this dysfunctional world. Our healing will be a means to the healing of the Church. Our selfishness will become selflessness. The addictive culture will find its denial broken as it is confronted with the truth, lived out radiantly by a body of believers.

What this may mean for the professional clergy is suggested by the experience of Bill Hybels, the pastor of the Willow Creek Community Church in Chicago. He found that people weren't attending church for a variety of reasons: "They always ask for money. I don't like the music. I can't relate to the message. The services are boring, predictable and irrelevant. The pastor makes me feel guilty and ignorant, so I leave feeling worse than when I came."[7] From 125 people fourteen years ago, the congregation has grown to more than 12,000. Hybels says that his goal is to reach the unchurched "Harrys and Marys who have been turned off by the traditional church and are about to write off Christianity."[8] In order to do this, Willow Creek has colorful, precisely planned multimedia services. He shares his success in three how-to conferences that attract over 1,500 pastors each year.

Hybels's success came with much personal cost. The stress of big time ministry brought him dangerously close to a break-down several years back. As a result he had to restructure his life. Russell Chandler writes in the *Los Angeles Times,*

> There's a tremendous price to keep what Hybels calls "the edge of excellence." Hybels readily acknowledges his high intensity and strict discipline. He usually arrives at his office between five and six each morning, lifts weights and runs two to four miles a day; fasts several days a week; and eats health foods.

Chandler reports that he gets regular rest, physical exercise, spiritual reflection, time off with his family, and personal accountability. Today, according to Chandler, "He informally reports to three male confidantes who, he says, would tell him in a 'heartbeat' if he strayed off the track."[9]

Basically, Hybels is in recovery from the addictive culture and the addictive church. His relationship with Jesus and accountability to his family and close friends guard him from relapsing in the midst of a high profile ministry. What an example!

Putting It All Together

As we follow the Twelve Steps with Jesus, we will become more functional. *Fear will go* as we give up trying to control our lives, let down our false fronts, face our false selves, and become honest about our moral failures. Fear will go as we expose what we have done to other people and what we have allowed them to do to us. Fear will go as we allow God to come into our lives and remove our sense of abandonment and our shame base. Fear will go as we detach from the addictive objects that have enslaved us.

Freedom will come as we receive God's forgiveness for our past, repent of our failures, and set others free when we forgive them. Freedom will come as Jesus fills us with his love, setting us free to love others in nonaddictive and nonmanipulative ways.

Self-giving will be the result of freedom from fear. We will make amends to those whom we have wronged and share our new lives with them. We will offer others what we've found in a real relationship with Jesus—a way out of our addictions and codependencies. In this new self-giving lifestyle are adventures and staggering challenges. Here are lives worth living to the hilt. We are no longer on lonely islands, but in communities where our deepest needs will be met, deepest desires supported, and broadest visions fulfilled.

Part Four

A Functional
Fellowship

. . .

Chapter 11

A Fearless Church

.   .   .

O nce we've received God's unconditional love, we're faced with a crisis. The addictive culture and the addictive church continue to undermine our experiences of that love. Like alcoholics, other addicts can not be isolated from their families. While they're the perceived patients, their whole family units are really sick or "dysfunctional." Every member is affected by the addictive disease and plays out his or her role accordingly. Because of this dysfunction, families have to be brought into the process of recovery.

Let's apply this insight to the life of the Church.

How can we grow in grace if we're parts of communities filled with "shoulds" and "oughts" that help to keep us sick? We're like recovering alcoholics trying to stay sober in a bar. Recently, a friend of mine confessed his moral inventory to a local priest, who is a sober alcoholic. The priest then offered him absolution. He went on to tell my friend not to come to church for a while, warning, "There is too much guilt here. It will endanger your recovery."

Millions of people who profess to be born again find themselves estranged from the institutional Church. Apart from their own personal issues of unbelief and disobedience to God, many must maintain their independence from the Church if they want a real, rather than a cultural relationship with Jesus. They instinctively avoid the fear-driven, addictive process of congregational life. As a Hollywood producer said to me when I was teaching a Bible class at a prestigious congregation, "I receive more acceptance from my non-Christian friends in the industry than I do from my Christian friends at this church." Untold others sadly echo this statement deep in their hearts.

This is a crisis not only for the Church, but also for people who need what the Church has to offer. They need its worship. They need to hear the Word of God and receive the sacraments. They need prayer. They need healing and support in their pain. They need to learn to study the Bible. They need other Christians to love them and to invest in their lives. Their children need to be raised to know Jesus. They need companions in order to impact this world for Christ. They need to pursue justice in the world. We were created to be together; no wonder all of the biblical images for the Church are corporate. We are living stones being built into the temple of God. We've been enlisted into the army of Christ and adopted into the family of God. We are to call each other "brother" and "sister," accordingly.

The concept of the family of God only makes sense in functional relationships. Confusion reigns in the Church when theory and practice collide. When we get a straight message from the Bible and mixed messages from the Church, it drives us crazy. If we're living in addictive communities with codependent relationships, then we will never grow up into maturity, regardless of what we read. As a result, we will miss God's purpose to repopulate the planet with representations of himself.

Psychologists have concluded that our values only survive when they are reinforced by our behavior and primary relationships. Otherwise, they become meaningless. For example, if we say that we value honesty but are continually dishonest, then this value is nonfunctional. If we deceive and manipulate people, avoid confrontations, repress our true feelings out of fear, and operate from our shame bases, then it doesn't matter what we say about the truth. We are liars. For us to maintain the value of honesty, we need to be in honest relationships. If we don't live in this truth, we must repent and confess our lapses. If the Church doesn't demand transparency, then it simply reinforces the deception of our addictive culture, leading to our slow deaths.

Surrounded by dysfunction, we must practice the Twelve Steps for the rest of our lives. Our recovery will only be complete in heaven. In this sense, recovery is nothing less than a life of discipleship. But it must be lived in a recovering Church.

What Howard Snyder wrote fifteen years ago is even more true today: "For a radical gospel (the biblical kind) we need a radical church (the biblical kind). For the ever-new wine we must continually have new wineskins. In short, we need a cataclysm."[1] The old skins of the addictive church are hard and brittle. They quickly crack when God pours out the life of his Spirit into them. New wineskins hold a fearless church, alive to growth, change, and transformation.

If the fearless Jesus has his way, he will make us fearless in our relationships with him and each other. We will also be fearless in our confrontations with the world. As Paul said in Romans 8:15, "God has not given us a spirit of bondage to bring us back into fear again, but a spirit of sonship by which we cry out, 'Abba, Father.'" This verse shows us that we've been adopted into the heart of the Father. Through our adoption, the enemy is overcome, the gulf between us and God is bridged, the bondage of the law is broken, and intimacy is restored. Possessing this knowledge, we must banish fear. Fear has to do with punishment, but Jesus has taken our punishment on the cross. As a result, God's "perfect love casts out fear" (1 John 4:18). If we have remaining fears, they are not from Him. He "has not given us a spirit of fear, but [the Holy Spirit] of power, of love, and of self-control" (2 Tim. 1:7).

How can we be released from our fears as we journey together? First, we need to establish Christ-centered communities where all can find their true identities in submission to

God. Only his presence removes the shame and resulting fears of people's lives. Moreover, we need to be with people who are literally in love with Jesus and want to build open, honest relationships with each other.

How will this new kind of community carry on its life? First, we can no longer support church structures that can function within the culture but are dysfunctional within the Gospel. Picture the typical Sunday morning at a typical church. We dress up in our Sunday best, masking our true selves, and arrive with other look-alikes. We're welcomed at the door by professional, plastic smiles and handed a bulletin that has the service neatly laid out in advance. We sit for an hour in hard pews facing the back of other people's heads. We struggle through unsingable hymns that were written for other times and cultures. During the three minutes of the "ritual of friendship," we awkwardly greet those around us. We then listen to a twenty-five minute homily or inspirational word. After the benediction, we file out to greet a few friends while drinking tasteless coffee. Finally, we make a getaway so we can enjoy the rest of the day. This scenario is an old, highly controlled, fear-based ritual that needs to change. Where do we find new wineskins?

Fearless Worship

Real worship focuses on God. As we understand the true character of God, we want to offer him our love and gratitude. Through this process, we begin to let go of our attachments and the fear of losing them. Practically, this means that worship for the 1990s should be found in praise. Worshipful praise won't be restricted to the choir loft; it will be found in the pews as well. God wants the whole congregation to be his choir, not just a few professionals who "inspire" us with anthems offered to God on our behalf. He wants to receive worship and praise directly. For instance, rather than singing "He is Lord," we can all sing together, "You are Lord." The pronoun shift may seem minor, but when we sing "He is Lord," we are addressing each other rather than God. When we sing "You are Lord," our worship is expressed directly. We are acknowledging, individually and collectively, that we're in relationship with our Lord. Hymns about God are still needed for exhortation and edification, but they have to take a backseat to songs of direct praise and intimacy.

Whether in a free church or liturgical setting, worshipful praise should also be sustained, moving uninterrupted from one praise song to another. This gives us time to be released from distractions and self-preoccupation. It also gives the Holy Spirit time to come and begin to bless us and speak to us. In my own church it's common for us to sing together for over a half an hour. We give God time to speak to our hearts. Praise builds as we move from song to song. Little by little, our thoughts become focused on his greatness and mercy. This kind of worship is theologically correct, spiritually satisfying, and culturally relevant. Today, churches minister to the MTV generation, raised on rock music and rock concerts. They're also ministering to adults who, twenty years ago, spent several days camping out at Woodstock, 500,000 strong. Three hymns and an anthem satisfies neither them nor the God who they're learning to love. Appropriate solos and choir selections can support congregational praise but should never be a substitute for it.

In a true Church service, worship is no longer viewed as an "opening exercise" but rather as an intensely spiritual and personal experience. Rather than being a mere preliminary to a sermon, worship becomes an event in and of itself. There are moments when the worshipers are literally overcome by the presence of God.

Church is participatory; people no longer sit as spectators, waiting for someone to entertain them. Each individual worshiper has his or her place before God's throne.

As we engage in corporate praise, healing and evangelism will result. Worship will become a weapon of God's kingdom in our warfare against Satan. God, in his sovereignty, will respond to our open welcome of him into our midst.

As individuals in this kind of worship, we focus on God, considering his beauty, power, and compassion. This draws us outside of ourselves where our fears begin to flee; God's perfect love falls on us and casts out fear. Instead of feeling abandoned, our faith is restored, joy is released, repentance and cleansing become real. As we find our identity in God's presence, we move toward our ultimate destiny—to become like him.

I have a friend who was in a church several years ago where the worship became so intense that people spontaneously went down the aisle to accept Jesus. Encountering the presence of God, they had to know him then and there. No sermon had been preached or invitation extended. This was real worship that rolled back the darkness and brought people into the light.

Fearless Preaching

In a functional fellowship, preaching is, once again, filled with the crucified and risen Jesus. The cross is restored to its rightful center of theology and faith. The cross is, as James Denney said years ago, "the diamond pivot on which the whole system of Christian truth revolves."[2] Within the body of a sermon, events and inspirational niceties fade before the cross's all encompassing, commanding reality.

Preaching the word of Christ crucified was scandalous and liberating to the first-century world; it is the same to the world today. In our addictive culture, with its dishonesty, selective memory, and manipulated images, the cross contains an offensive message that is easily forgotten or repressed. The cross confronts humanity's reason and conscience, leaving it speechless. It also presents people with the possibility for monumental rejection. No wonder the cross is either avoided entirely or reduced to a gold-plated theology.

To the world, the cross is a philosophical offense. It is offensive because it's particular. Rather than simply illustrating the universal truth of God's love, the cross established that truth. When Jesus of Nazareth suffered under Pontius Pilate outside the walls of Jerusalem, he was nailed up on Roman boards at a particular time and place. This event *was* love, not merely an act of love. The event of the cross continues to be love. Only through the cross can we know of God's open heart toward us. Only in the cross do God's holiness and love "kiss," as Luther said. The cross shows us the unconditional love of the Father through his Son who bears away our sins and makes salvation available to the whole world. In 1 John 4:10 we read: "In this is love, not that we loved God, but that He loved us and sent His Son to be the propitiation for our sins." Similarly, Paul said in Romans 5:8, "But God demonstrates His own love toward us, in that while we were yet sinners, Christ died for us."

For myself, I would do anything to get around this philosophical offense. In my flesh, I hate to say that Jesus is the only way to God, that there is no other name given among men by which we must be saved. My reason is offended by this. My false sense of fairness balks at this. What about all those who have never heard the Gospel? What about those who are sincere in their faiths? What about Buddha and Gandhi? To even try to answer these questions here would dilute the point. The point is the offense of the particular—one name, one way, one Mediator, one Savior, one atonement, one King. Jesus is Lord.

There is also a historical offense in the cross. A Jewish carpenter, legally executed under Roman law, is the Savior of the world. Justin Martyr describes the offence caused by the cross as "madness." He writes, "They say that our *madness* consists in the fact that we put a *crucified man* in second place after the unchangeable and eternal God, the Creator of the world."[3] Professor Martin Hengel notes that by proclaiming the crucified Jesus as the eternal Son of God, the scandal of Christianity "was immeasurably increased."[4] He further concludes,

> There may have been many crucified righteous men in the ancient world. . . . But for Jews and Greeks the crucified Son of God was an unheard-of idea. . . . The discrepancy between the shameful death of a Jewish state criminal and the confession that depicts this executed man as a preexistent divine figure who becomes man and humbles himself to a slave's death is, as far as I can see, without analogy in the ancient world.[5]

How easy it is for me to cover the cross with Christian platitudes. When have I been accused of madness? How often have I thrust home the point that the eternal, unchanging God was in Christ, bloody on the cross. I have weakened this fact by too much of a severe separation between the Father and the Son. I have often preached as if the Father passively and heartlessly watched the Son die, satisfying his justice and upholding his Law against sinners, while Jesus became an innocent third party. No! The Father *in* the Son bears away our sins. In the cross is the full suffering love of the Godhead. This isn't just a good idea. This isn't a myth. This is the historical event that determines all of history from start to finish.

Closely linked to the cross's historical offense is a cultural offense. The cross was despised in antiquity. Detractors of the Christian message called it folly. In *Crucifixion,* Martin Hengel again reveals that the cross was not even a topic for conversation in polite society. Under Roman law, crucifixion was the supreme penalty, even above decapitation and burning, since it included humiliation, torture, and death. Normally, no Roman citizen could be crucified. The cross was called "the infamous stake" and "the criminal wood." It was reserved to terrorize slaves and subject people. When the Roman General Titus laid siege to Jerusalem, he crucified five hundred Jews each day around the walls of the city. The Stoic philosopher Seneca aptly summed up the prevailing attitude:

Can anyone be found who would prefer wasting away in pain dying limb by limb, or letting out his life drop by drop, rather than expiring once for all? Can any man be found willing to be fastened to the accursed tree, long sickly, already deformed, swelling with ugly weals on shoulders and chest, and drawing the breath of life amid long-drawn-out agony?[6]

The apostles' incredible message was that one man could be found who would chose such a death—Jesus. They didn't hush up the message of the cross like the addictive church's family secret. They confidently announced the news from the house-tops. In light of the Resurrection and the coming of the Spirit, they excitedly proclaimed that in the cross was found the salvation of the world.

Examining my heart, I must ask myself disturbing questions: How often have I been willing to speak vividly and boldly of Jesus' death? How willing have I been to bring it up in polite preaching or polite conversation? My Christianity is so nice and well defended. My abandonment and shame issue leads me to dodge the cultural offense of the cross. The scandal of the cross isn't merely for the ancient world, but for my generation as well. In an age of brutality, violence, and despair, isn't the brutality of Christ crucified the only solution that can claim our lasting attention? What I once heard Howard Kuist call the Book of Leviticus can be said of the whole Bible: "A bloody book for a bloody world."

After the cultural offense of the cross, there is a moral offense. This offense is the bottom line, because it confronts our pride and attachment to addictions. We cannot save ourselves. We cannot know God and get to heaven based on our intellect, virtue, or good works. All our self-sufficient efforts are filthy rags. We are saved only by the atoning death of Jesus, who hung on the cross in our place. In him, we now die to our false selves in order to enter a redeemed relationship with the living God. This is and will always be the message of the non-addictive Church. As Paul said in 1 Corinthians 1:22–24,

> For indeed Jews ask for signs, and Greeks search for wisdom; but we preach Christ crucified, to Jews a stumbling block, and to Gentiles foolishness, but to those who are the called, both Jews and Greeks, Christ is the power of God and the wisdom of God.

In the cross is my righteousness, or right-standing, before God. It was with this confidence that Paul could write in Romans 1:16–17,

> For I am not ashamed of the gospel. It is the power of God unto salvation for the Jew first and also the Greek. For in it the righteousness of God is revealed [as a gift], starting with faith and ending with faith. As it is written, "He who through faith is righteous shall live."

The Gospel is only complete, however, in the announcement that Jesus has been raised from the dead. It is the Resurrection that vindicates the Crucifixion as an act of God. The Resurrection assures us that the atoning work of Jesus is complete. It is the Resurrection that proclaims death has been conquered. The Resurrection gives us the ground to believe that Jesus is not locked into the past. We can know him personally today; he's our contemporary. James Denney writes,

> There can be no salvation from sin unless there is a living Savior: this explains the emphasis laid by the apostle [Paul] on the resurrection. But the Living One can only be a Savior because he has died: this explains the emphasis laid on the cross. The Christian believes in a living Lord, or he could not believe at all; but he believes in a living Lord who died an atoning death, for no other can hold the faith of a soul under the doom of sin.[7]

As the reality of the Resurrection gets into our guts, God will makes us fearless. Underlying our dread of rejection and abandonment is our dread of death. This is our ultimate and last enemy. As Ernest Becker writes, ". . . the idea of death, the fear of it, haunts the human animal like nothing else; it is a mainspring of human activity—activity designed largely to avoid the fatality of death, to overcome it by denying in some way that it is the final destiny for man."[8] Wait. Here is the good news. Jesus has taken our separation from God upon the cross and conquered death's final abandonment in his Resurrection. Now we can sing and shout for joy! He has taken our fear, making us free to live.

Fearless Community

A Christ-centered community is also a people-centered community because Jesus is fully human as well as fully divine. I once heard Dr. Bob Munger preach, "When we get close to Jesus' heart, we get close to the things that are on his heart, and what is on his heart is people." Both great commandments—to love God with everything that we have and to love our neighbor as ourselves—are fulfilled together. As Jesus, the one fully functional person, commands our lives, we become more and more functional in our relationships with him and with each other.

Because of this, our Christian communities can engage in fearless relationships where we detach from our addictions, drop our masks, and get real. We think what we think and say it, even if we're wrong. We feel what we feel and express it, even if our feelings are hostile and sinful. Only by exposing ourselves to each other in a safe environment can we be healed and forgiven.

By confessing our fears of being misunderstood, rejected, and abandoned to each other, we expose our human limitations and toxic shame bases. As our being wounds are revealed, they can be prayed for and healed by the presence of God.

Although we may feel unlovely, those feelings will be changed by Jesus' love for us and our resulting love for one another. Like Jesus, we will then be fearless in our ministry to the multitudes. We will be able to stop beside all the Jericho roads and tend to the dying. We will also be fearless toward our enemies. We will rejoice that we are able to suffer for Jesus' sake.

What will be the wineskins for this new resurrected and functioning wine?

In many congregations today, the action has shifted from larger services to informal home groups. Such groups are nothing new. Without professional clergy, buildings, Sunday schools, or Bibles, the New Testament Church grew through house churches. (See Paul's letter to Philemon.) In times of renewal, such as the eighteenth-century Wesleyan awakening, small groups have been key factors for serious Christians. In the midst of a technological, depersonalized, and addictive culture, with its resulting breakdown of the nuclear family, a new day has come for smaller intimate fellowships.

What are the practical values of small groups? Howard Snyder finds eight advantages in their design. First, this structure is flexible, easily accommodating changes in format and leadership. Second, small groups are mobile, moving easily from place to place. Third, they're inclusive. Without putting on their Sunday best, all can be welcomed and accommodated. Fourth, small groups are personal. Everyone is seen and known; people are missed when they don't attend. Fifth, they can grow by division. When the group gets too large it can easily split. Sixth, they can be effective means of evangelism. Many who will not come to a church building, will come to a small group. Seventh, they require minimal professional leadership. As these groups proliferate, lay leaders will have to raise up to lead them. Eighth, they are adaptable to the institutional Church. In fact a small group structure can become the basis for lay people effectively pastoring a large congregation through face-to-face weekly meetings.[9]

As we gather in small groups, we can get down to business. Worship becomes intimate. Bible study becomes personal and relevant. Since we're missed when we're not there, the lost biblical themes of discipline and accountability are recovered. In this setting, we may experience the presence and gifts of the Holy Spirit.

All Christians affirm some spiritual gifts—such as pastoring, teaching, exhortation, evangelism, leadership, acts of mercy, administration, and service. (See Rom. 12:3–8; Eph. 4:11–12.) It is my conviction that if we also welcome the Holy Spirit to come in fullness and give the Spirit time, we will begin to experience gifts such as prophecy, in which God speaks directly through impressions, Scripture, inner voices, visions, and dreams; healings through the laying on of hands and direct prayer for the sick; miracles, which are sheer supernatural, instantaneous interventions of God; discernment of good and evil spirits; and tongues, unintelligible prayer language that edifies our spirits. (See 1 Cor. 12 and 14.) What is so scary about spiritual gifts is that we must give up control in order to welcome the Spirit's control.

Rather than being fear based we must become faith based. We must be so Spirit-controlled that we will also be willing to risk nothing happening. Home groups are the perfect setting to take such risks. We must be comfortable with waiting on the Spirit in silence. We must be willing to be wrong or foolish and get out of the way so that the Spirit can move in our midst. We must be willing to step out when we feel the Spirit's nudging. Spiritual gifts must be exercised biblically, for the building up of the body, rather than for personal recognition. They must be used in love, rather than in competition and pride. If spiritual gifts are allowed to flourish, true body life grows, and people come together with fresh excitement, wondering what God will do in their group this week.[10]

Most important, home groups provide the setting to actualize Jesus' promise in John 13:35 that Christians will be known as his disciples because of their love for one another. When seven to twelve people gather and want to be real, the masks come off. Fears can be exposed. Shame can be healed. Emotional bonding can take place. People can pray honestly and realistically for each other. They can follow up on what happens in church services by informal contact through the week. In this setting, relationships rather than programs become the focus. Opportunities for outreach into the surrounding community will emerge. Here new people and older believers can be quickly united. What is the budget impact? Zero.

The multiplication of these groups forces the clergy to give up control. (After all, they can't be everywhere at once.) As this happens, addictive issues may surface once again for those of us in professional ministry. We can no longer simply be "fathers" and "mothers" in the Church, creating strings of dependent relationships and compulsively meeting every need of our "family." We can no longer be obsessed with fear-based control. This only fosters impossible expectations that set us up for people's anger and disappointment. We, in turn, keep them from finding God as their real "Abba," since they have us as an idolatrous substitute. We need to see ourselves more as coaches. It's our job to train lay leadership, putting each member into the game. We should instruct them in the basics and help them find their playing positions. We can coach them, discipline them, correct them, encourage them, and help them to improve, but we cannot and must not play the game for them. If we do, we will make them passive and, in effect, steal their ministries from them. This looks good for pastoral job security, but debilitates the Church, leaving pastors with dependent, anemic people. Instead, as we train leaders and release them to smaller cells of life, the whole body will grow.

Jesus must be our ministry example. Fearless about his message and mission, he trained his followers by always speaking the truth and sharing his true feelings with them. He was their fixed reference point. He risked entrusting his ministry into their hands. Pastors must do likewise. Small groups are a major vehicle for extending Jesus' kingdom work to others.

Small groups promote the emergence of new biblical leadership. These leaders aren't elected to administrative posts that perpetuate institutions. Rather, they emerge as they are called by God, as in the New Testament model. They actually shepherd the sheep by becoming their personal pastors. They teach and exhort those entrusted to their care. Their lives are examples to the flock because they minister in their own homes where people can see how they live "off-stage." Like the professional clergy, they become coaches too, carefully placing their people in the game at the right positions. "Ordination" as elders or pastors only confirms what the Lord has already done by raising them up as charismatic leaders and gracing them to submit to each other and to the body of Christ.

Led by both professionals and nonprofessionals, the Church can become more like the first-century Church—largely a lay movement through which pastoral care and discipleship have some context and meaning in people's lives. Through home groups, intimacy is restored in the Church. The whole body of Christ is marshaled for ministry because everyone can find his or her place. My friend Ford Madison proposes that as God restores the Church, the twentieth century, like the first century, will be known as the century of the laity. I believe he's right.

My first small-group experience came when I was a freshman in college through the ministry of Donn Moomaw. He had been an all-American linebacker and had used his influence to witness through Billy Graham's worldwide ministry. He was on his way to Princeton Seminary when he stopped in Colorado to visit Dawson Trotman, the founder of the Navigators. Dawson remarked about Donn's ministry and then asked, "But where are your Donn Moomaws? How are you reproducing your life in others?" As a result of this challenge, Donn gathered a small group of Princeton Seminary and University students for prayer and Bible study every Friday morning at six A.M. I was a part of this small group. There, my love for the Word of God was forged. It was a warm, open fellowship that helped me keep my eyes on Jesus, which sustained me in a hostile academic environment. This group was an alternative to a legalistic group of other Christians who played on my insecurities and threatened my freedom in Christ. Donn Moomaw's small group of friends aided me in the larger, celebrative, Sunday worship services. I am confident that such small groups will do the same for all of us today.

Small groups are also part of the answer for breaking generational and environmental sin. God not only wants to restore our personal relationships with himself, but also wants to place us in new families where we will learn how to become functional with each other. In small groups, our relationships with Jesus are reinforced by new brothers and sisters who mirror growing, healthy, biblical lives. Here we are able to deal with our "stuff." Rather than receiving condemnation from the enemy, we receive conviction from the Spirit. As confession of sin and cleansing are mediated through our fellow believers, repentance becomes real, creating lasting changes. Accountability is another result of small groups. As we grow through accountability, the fear that covers up our shame bases will begin to dissolve.

God intended the Church to be without fear, legalism, and judgment. We can have such churches where speaking the truth in love makes us grow up into Christ, churches where we don't let the sun go down on our anger toward each other. We can have churches where we don't give the devil any opportunities in our lives. We can be free to be tenderhearted, forgiving each other as God in Christ has forgiven us. Our churches can be places where not even the suspicion of a sinfull lifestyle will be seen because darkness will be exposed. Our churches can be places where we sing to each other with songs and hymns, and spiritual songs, building each other up in worship and praise. Most important, we can submit to each other out of our awe of Christ. (For the scriptural description of the fully functional Church, see Ephesians 4, 5, and 6.)

The functional Church is also where our marriages and families are redeemed. Rather than continuing the poisonous pedagogy of our upbringing, which was based on law, husbands will love their wives as Christ loved the Church, and wives, in turn, will freely submit to the love of Jesus given to them through their husbands. This creates the spiritual and emotional environment in which healthy children are raised. For children to obey their parents in this environment doesn't mean submitting to a continuing chain of abuse. It means obeying their parents in the Lord. (See Eph. 6:1.) Jesus inhabits the center of a family that is increasingly nonaddictive. He pours his love into parents and children who are learning to detach their compulsive desires from each other. In this way, they can love each other genuinely from their hearts. The Bible finally starts to make sense in this kind of environment.

The functional Church not only builds healthy communities and families but also confronts the evils of this world. Having died to its "people pleasing," it is no longer silent about the demonic bondages that oppress people, physically and spiritually. Rather than being preoccupied with the liberal agendas for social action, the Church calls for intercessory prayer to break the spiritual strongholds over cities and individuals. Rather than using toxic religion in order to flee from the suffering in this world, the Church endures people's pain for the sake of their redemption and healing. This will lead to radical witnessing and to acts of mercy that will challenge the surrounding, entrenched power structure with a demand for social justice.

In my own church, members have been called to minister to the homeless in Mission Beach near San Diego. We set up a store, and the Lord clearly told us to freely give away all the food and clothes we collect rather than run a thrift shop. He promised us that as we did so, we would have endless supplies.

This has proven to be the case. We have served untold hundreds of people. Many customers are flabbergasted because the clothes and bags of food are free. This is a ministry founded in prayer and divine direction. It's the embodiment of the message of free grace that we proclaim. Through this ministry the poor are clothed and fed; many come seeking prayer as well. They pick up Bibles and become a part of a new Church that God is calling into being.

Our ministry in Mission Beach challenges the business establishment in the surrounding community. Property owners are concerned that we will attract the "undesirable" homeless to the area, even through the homeless have been there for years. Business people are unsure about the impact of free clothes and food on their patrons. This sets us up for potential harassment. As Christians we're not to provoke hostility, but we must be ready for it when it comes. Could Jesus have had similar problems when some men ripped up a roof to bring their paralyzed friend to him? If pressure from the world mounts, we can live out another aspect of the Gospel—loving our enemies and praying for those who persecute us in Jesus' name.

As the fearless Jesus deals with us, our denial works less and less. We are lead to worship God and center our lives in him with praise. We must preach the cross with boldness and suffer the consequences. We must be honest with ourselves and with each other. This leads us to build person-centered communities and families. As we face the sea of need around us, we must be prepared to risk suffering and counterattacks from the kingdom of darkness. No matter what happens, we can be prepared for battle, for our identities and destinies are secure. Jesus' perfect love has cast out all our fears.

Chapter 12

A Freeing Church

.   .   .

T he addictive process begins to break up within the life of
the Christian community when our fears are exposed
and we are restored to vital relationships with God and
with each other. Secure in God's love, we no longer have to lie,
manipulate, or try to control each other in order to fill the holes
in our souls. The basis for true Christian community is found in
relationship with the Lord Jesus Christ, the one really fearless
and free person. Jesus liberates us from our old, addictive lives
with all of their bondages. He liberates each of us for the new
life that we can only find in him. Jesus also places us in relationship to a Christian community where we can become the people that God has created us to be.

Jesus has come to set both individual persons and his whole
Church free from the devil, the world (the addictive culture),
the law (perfectionism), idolatry (our attachments), and the
flesh (our false selves). Through Jesus we are freed from the
need to perform in order to be accepted by God or each other.
Jesus frees us to surrender ourselves to the Father's will and
find our identity and destiny together in him. We are free to
love God with all that we are and our neighbors as ourselves.
The truth we receive from Jesus frees us to liberate others from
bondage. These new-found freedoms that Jesus offers transform the way we live our individual lives as well as the way the
Christian community lives together as God's people.

Freedom in Worship

God is God of order, not of mood altering, Dionysian frenzy
(1 Cor. 14:40). We are to love God with our minds as well as our
hearts, and through our worship, the church is to be built up.
But, while order is important, the Holy Spirit is meant to be
free in true worship. Such worship sets us free from controlling, predictable, and perfectionistic worship patterns and sets
us free to enjoy the living God, to expect him to do something
fresh and new for this particular people, at this particular hour,
on this particular Sunday. Even our body language can reflect
our freedom. We are free to sit quietly, stand, or kneel. We are
free to laugh, sing, weep, or dance. We are free to fold our
hands or to lift our hands. What God is doing in each one's
heart in the moment can take physical form, as long as it doesn't
distract others from their own encounters with God.

In my church we are now free for what is called the "Song
of the Lord." During our regular worship, the Holy Spirit often
gives sung prophetic messages through gifted and anointed
worship leaders. These prophetic words come in the form of
prayers, scriptural meditations, or words of direct address from
God to the people. Spirit-led worship is liberated. It is not
haphazard but planned and prayed for by strong leaders who
are sensitive to the Spirit. Out of this security, there is an ensuing openness and confidence to take some risks that allow freedom and responsiveness from God's people.

As we participate in spontaneous worship, many of us may
rediscover our "lost child," the emotionally expressive and
childlike part of us that was shut down long ago. Alice Miller
says that when we see people laughing and crying, we are
often threatened by their emotional display. Our initial reaction is to stop them, unconsciously trying to curb our own
childlike impulses that are being mirrored back to us.[1] We
want to abuse the expressive child just as we were abused. We

want to regain control just as we were controlled. In our new experiences of Spirit-led worship we may instinctively want to stamp out any real display of joy or sorrow. This impulse to control emotional expression is a way to not face our own repressed childhood feelings.[2] If we can weather our discomfort, however, we may receive great healing. As we are freed up to worship in more heartfelt and childlike ways, we become whole. Spirit-led worship is part of the new gift that God is giving to us. Rather than fearing freedom (the old addictive mode), we need to welcome it as from him.

A church living in freedom needs also to be open to prophetic revelation. Rather than undermining the canon of Scripture, such words, dreams, and visions from the Spirit fulfill the scriptural promises that God continually will speak living words to us today. (See Acts 2; 1 Cor. 12.) Our openness to prophecy will only come as we deal with the addictive issues of our lives. By allowing the prophetic gifts to function in our churches, our controlling spirits are released from fear. We no longer are bound to linear thought patterns or a preset order of worship.

With the gift of prophecy in worship, divine direction can come during the service. More than once I have heard a current word from the Lord in the midst of worship, and I have been led to change my sermon in that very moment to respond to what God was saying. Another benefit of freedom in worship allows for a more lively and personal ministry with the congregation. For example, on a recent Sunday a couple was visiting us from the East Coast for the first time. Toward the end of the service, I asked for God to show us any needs for prayer. Kathy, one of our worship leaders who had never met these visitors, spoke out both of their first names and gave a directive word to them. Needless to say, they were shaken to the core as they came forward to receive prayer. It was a life-changing moment for them and exciting for us: We knew that the living God was in our midst. That experience was also a self-giving moment for Kathy as she stepped out in faith. In our church today, many people remain after the service to pray for each other and to take advantage of trained healing teams that minister to the sick.

One of the ironies of the evangelical church is that while it has held a "high" view of Scripture, insisting that the whole Bible is inspired by God and normative for daily life, evangelical Christians have been very selective as to what we use from Scripture in congregational life. A visiting Evangelical Free minister said to me recently, "My elders accept my belief that all the gifts of the Spirit are for the Church today as long as I don't teach about them or seek to minister in them." This pastor's obedience to God is now on the line.

Jesus, through his Spirit, wants to restore the whole of Scripture for the ministry of the Church. Through the Evangelical Movement, he has restored the Gospel of salvation by grace, the practical teaching of the epistles and the missionary mandate for world evangelism. Through the Pentecostal and Charismatic Movements, Jesus has restored the teaching on the Holy Spirit described in the Book of Acts and the gifts of the Spirit emphasized in Paul's letters. Through the Jesus Movement, he has restored the intimacy of worship found in the Psalms and the apocalyptic fervor of his return. Through John Wimber and the "Third Wave"[3] of the outpouring of the Holy Spirit, Jesus has restored the ministries of anointing, deliverance, healing, and love for the poor found in the Gospels. Through the Prophetic Movement, he has restored the practical value of Old Testament history and prophecy to the behavior of the church today.

Freedom in worship and ministry come not by abandoning the Bible but by giving the Bible its rightful authoritative and functional place in the life of the community. Freed from fear in Jesus, we are now free to express our whole-hearted obedience in worship.

Freedom in Preaching

As the Spirit moves, the Church will experience a freedom in communicating God's Word. I received classical training in preaching classes where I produced carefully crafted, written sermon manuscripts. The introduction had to grab people's attention. The body of the sermon was formed from three clear points. The conclusion was to be punched home with force to leave a memorable impression upon the hearers. Illustrations needed to be catchy and to relate to the various segments of the congregation. A medical illustration would impress the doctors. An athletic illustration would appeal to the men. An illustration from family life would touch traditional women. And so it went. All of these goals were to be achieved in about twenty minutes. The congregation's attention span was assumed to disappear after that.

As I reflected upon this plan for preaching, I realized that the communicators who touched me didn't follow it to the letter. In school, I really enjoyed my professors' lectures when they diverged from their notes and spoke to the passions in their hearts. Often the sermons that I remembered most were those that broke homiletical rules. I recalled Billy Graham pacing a platform, Bible in hand, preaching with an authority that closely following a written manuscript could never allow. I still believe that all preaching demands careful preparation. Yet preparation blended with an openness to the Spirit provides a sure foundation out of which inspiration comes in the moment of delivery. In the words of John Mackay, the former president of Princeton Seminary, "order will give way to ardor."

As I teach the Bible to my people, there are moments when the Holy Spirit comes upon me, and I experience an anointing from God alone. The gift that God gives has nothing to do with possessing a charismatic personality. True inspiration has nothing to do with emotional manipulation, nor will it cover up for a lack of preparation. The power to deliver anointed sermons comes from sound preparation and an openness to the Spirit.

This is why Paul tells the Corinthians that he was among them with much fear and trembling. Paul was totally human and fully ready to admit his weakness. He never presented himself as preacher perfect. The Corinthians saw Paul's weaknesses, and they felt God's anointing upon him. Thus they gave the glory to God. Paul writes,

> And my message and my preaching were not in persuasive words of wisdom, but in demonstration of the Spirit and of power, that your faith should not rest on the wisdom of men, but on the power of God. (1 Cor. 2:4–5)

Only Paul's kind of preaching is consistent with the proclamation of the cross. The scandal of Christ crucified in weakness must be born by weak messengers. At the same time, through these humble people the Spirit releases the very power of God to those who are "being saved" (1 Cor. 1:21–24). Through this power we know that God himself has come!

God wants to give every preacher this freedom. The Church yearns for it. Here's how to receive this gift: Prepare more than usual. Pray like mad. Abandon the bondage of a manuscript. (Let the fear go, and give up the need to control.) Ask the Spirit to come. Get close to the people. Even abandon the pulpit if necessary. Sustain eye contact. Let your whole body speak. Be faithful to the biblical text, be honest, and then take a step of faith. Be willing to fail. See what God will do.

Freedom in Community

The discovery of real community through informal fellowships or home groups is another demonstration of freedom. In small groups our freedom is reinforced by those who also have been liberated. Here we discover our new family. Rather than suffering in our old dysfunctional patterns, we begin to experience healthy relationships. No wonder Jesus promises us new brothers and sisters and fathers and mothers in his kingdom. At last, we are free to say what we think and feel what we feel. We are free to love our neighbors as ourselves.

The values that form the core of God's family are liberating values. First, we enjoy the *authority of being adopted* into God's family. We are free from alienation; we are free to belong. John promises us that we receive legal rights as God's children when we are reborn by the Spirit (John 1:12). Paul says we are now joint-heirs with Christ (Rom. 8:17). All that is God's is ours. As I have experienced more and more of God's love, I've learned that my birthright includes powerful encounters with the Holy Spirit, deep inner healing, a personal relationship with the Word of God, and real answers to my prayers. The adventure of living by faith has given me victory over the kingdom of darkness, and the leadership of the Holy Spirit has offered me the joy of seeing God use me in some measure in the lives of people around me. My birthright also includes patient endurance, provision in suffering, and a hope that does not disappoint me.

Second, in God's family we find *a new identity*. We are free from being displaced persons in this world. We were lost; now we are found. We now have one Father, and we are all brothers and sisters. We have the privilege of greeting each other with a "holy kiss" (1 Cor. 16:20). As a teenager I struggled with peer acceptance. After becoming a Christian, I was warmly welcomed into God's family. For the first time I felt I belonged. Fellow students whom I admired greeted me with smiles and hugs. Like the prodigal, I had come home; I felt accepted, and there was a party for me. Over the years, these greetings have been repeated again and again. Jesus is the tie that binds us together beyond race and culture.

Third, we have *a new security*. Home has been defined as "where they have to take you in." As members of God's family we've been given the key to the entire kingdom! In God's family we know that we belong. This facilitates our becoming more and more functional. We can risk speaking our thoughts and feelings because ultimate rejection or abandonment is gone. Our family security becomes concrete as we exercise the gift of hospitality toward each other. We open our homes as well as our hearts. At times, God allows us to offer a refuge for a new believer who needs the physical security of a safe environment. At times, we may be called upon to take in the homeless. As we offer even a cup of cold water in Jesus' name, we extend God's welcome to others who seek a place of comfort.

Fourth, in our new family we must *live honestly* by respecting each other's thoughts and feelings. We are free from the old lies, the old deceptions. We are free to know ourselves and each other. At last, there is no abusive control over our emotions. There is no "party line" to parrot. We learn the truth from Jesus; we tell it to each other, and he sets us free.

As a freshman in college I found myself involved with a highly structured small group of legalistic Christians. Unconsciously, I spent much of my Christian life devoted to winning their acceptance. I became a confrontive evangelist in order to score points with my closed circle of friends. Sadly, I was emotionally cut off from the feelings and real needs of the unbelievers I sought to win. On my flight back to California at the end of the school year, I sat beside a woman traveling to Hawaii to deal with her father's death. I immediately thought, "I must witness to this woman." Yet my next thought unnerved me, "I don't want to witness to this woman because I don't have any of my friends with me to tell that I did so." I sunk into a reflective silence for the rest of the flight. I realized that most of my Christian life for the past year had been motivated out of fear and the need for peer approval. My insecurities had hidden me from my own motives. In my private agony, I knew that I had to change. I had to become honest, and I needed a new family that would truly value and accept me.

Fifth, we live together in a nurturing environment that is determined by *love.* Paul tells us that this love builds up (1 Cor. 8:1). Love is emotional support undergirded by tenderheartedness and kindness that seeks our good alone. I recall my shock some years ago when Ted, an undergraduate at the University of Southern California, made an appointment to see me. He came into my office, sat down, and said, "I have come to find out how you are." Ted didn't want anything from me. He didn't want a personal problem solved or a theological question answered. He didn't want a job or a reference to graduate school. He didn't want money. He simply wanted to know how I was. For a few minutes I couldn't believe that he was serious. Had he made an appointment only with my welfare in mind? Suddenly I felt overwhelmed. I experienced an unforgettable loving moment.

Sixth, God's family life includes *discipline.* We are free from the old self-destructive chaos. We are free for a new sense of responsibility. The boundaries of God's will and purpose for us are established. His moral order is honored. This is not legalism since it is predicated upon the change that God has worked in our hearts. I recall having to confront a brother in regard to his relationship with a woman in our church. Unmarried, they were sexually active. I knew that I could lose both of them from our family over this. Yet my love for Jesus and for them compelled me to act. As this man and I talked, I affirmed my love for him and confessed my fears. I truthfully told him that what I had to say was difficult for me. I admitted that I had worried about his reaction. Tears came and we both wept. Love triumphed. The sexual relationship was ended. Spiritual health was restored and much personal growth resulted for both this man and woman.

Seventh, in the family of God we *care for each other's physical needs.* We are free to give. If we have material goods we share them freely (1 John 3:17). Christian love has no strings attached. This love, concretely given, expects nothing in return.

This is the love that comes from God. I experienced this love some years ago when a lawyer friend from Houston called to find out how I was doing. When I shared my financial dilemma with him, which was impacting my vocational future, unsolicited checks began to arrive regularly. He helped my wife and me through an extended time of difficulty, never asking us to account for the funds he sent. His love and trust freed us to follow God's direction and kept us more accountable than the I.R.S. ever could.

Eighth, rather than sick dependency, our family goal is to *grow up into maturity.* This means achieving a healthy interdependency. We will become functional adults together; reproductions of the very image of God in this world. Out of our full life in Christian community and by the power of God's Spirit within us, we are free to express Jesus' life in this world.

Freedom for the World

Jesus revealed his agenda for ministry in his sermon in Nazareth. With the anointing of his Spirit upon him, he was to preach the gospel to the poor, set the captives free, heal the sick, and liberate the oppressed. Jesus' agenda must also become our agenda. Like Jesus, we must become *relationally free.* We are not to remain in or become attached to addictive relationships. We are not to use people to shore up our egos or our church programs. We are to see beyond the costumes, the masks, the disguises others may wear. We are willing to risk rejection for Jesus' sake. When we see people's hurts, we suffer with them. Their relationship with Jesus is more important to us than their ability to meet our needs, finance our programs, or pick up the tab for lunch. We will become, as my pastor friend Dick Langford says "the only institution that exists for its nonmembers."

We must also become *economically free.* Most of us are not called to an itinerant ministry. We go to work unless we're still in school, at home with children, disabled, or retired. At the same time, job security is not meant to become an idol. A few years ago when I was asked to resign from my church, I was forced to discover anew who I was in Christ. I reexamined my commitment to the renewal of the church. If keeping my job and belonging to the pension fund had been my highest values, then I would have fought for my position. My integrity would have been compromised. As one born during the Depression in the 1930s, I must continually turn my financial fears and attachments over to the Lord and let them go.

As God sets us free economically, one of the greatest objections to the Gospel is overcome. People begin to believe that we are not in ministry for the money. We won't manipulate others in order to see what we can get out of them. If our kingdom is not of this world and our treasures are in heaven, we are happy to give our money away to extend Jesus' ministry in the world. At the same time, we won't simply throw money at the needs around us but will give as well of ourselves to meet the world's sorrows.

Next, like Jesus, we are *socially free*. Being with God and hearing from him draws us away from the clamor of this world and then reinvests us back into it for his sake. For example, my friend Jim Green met with the Minister of Tourism for a Caribbean country recently. As they talked, the Minister kept moving in and out of his office. Confusion reigned. As Jim silently prayed about the situation, God said, "Tell him to shut the door." So Jim simply said, "Shut the door." The Minister looked surprised and asked, "Why?" The Lord then said, "Tell him that he is troubled and busy and that I have told you to pray with him." The Minister then shut the door and sat down. Jim read several Psalms to him. As he did so, the Minister began to weep; his heart was opened. Jim's intimacy with God moved him into bold, effective ministry. This is what Jesus wants to do with all of us. Once we are spiritually free, we can give ourselves away.

Jesus has come to set us free. As we live with Jesus, we become freer and freer ourselves. We are liberated from the addictions and compulsions that bind us. We are free to authentically love each other. We are free to become part of a church that freely worships God. We will find a new freedom in welcoming the gifts of the Spirit into our midst. We will find ourselves growing in a functional fellowship where we are nurtured in the freedom that Jesus has for us. New family values are learned and reinforced as we move out into the world to express Jesus' love to those who do not know him. Increasingly freed from bondage to our addictions, we are free for each other and for this world. As a result, the Gospel is incarnated in our lives as the only alternative to our consumptive culture. We become a part of the Church that is setting people free.

Chapter 13

A Self-Giving Church

. . .

ddicts live consumptive lives; they are users. Jesus is exactly the opposite—he sets us free to reflect his self-giving in our relationships with God and with each other. How will this happen?

Self-Giving Worship

In the addictive church, people come to worship in order to get rather than to give. As users, their preoccupation is, "What's in it for me? Do I enjoy the aesthetics? Are people friendly to me? Do I like the music? Am I inspired by the choir? Does the preaching feed me? Is the pastor friendly? Does the pastor know my name?" Such pious expectations about our spiritual growth barely hide our full-blown narcissism. Often I hear people say, "I'm going to another church. My needs aren't being met here." Whatever the merits of this complaint, it has nothing to do with worship. The reason is simple.

Worship is not getting; worship is giving. The word *worship* in Hebrew means "to fall down, to surrender, to submit," as in a slave or subject bowing low before a mighty king. The word in Greek means "to come toward to kiss." This kiss is not an act of intimacy, it is an act of submission, as in kissing the ground before a sovereign, or kissing his feet.[1]

Worship is the basis for a life of self-giving; it is surrendering ourselves to God. Consider Psalm 95:6: "Come, let us worship and bow down; Let us kneel before the Lord our Maker," or Psalm 99:5: "Exalt the Lord our God, And worship at His footstool; Holy is He."

In the New Testament we are called to worship as priests. There is no clergy class. (See 1 Pet. 2:5.) All believers belong to this priesthood. Like Israel, we are not to come to God empty-handed. Slaughtered sheep, goats, or bulls, however, are no longer acceptable sacrifice. The last bloody sacrifice was made on the cross by Jesus. What then are we to bring?

First, as priests, we are to give God our bodies. They bear our whole selves. As Paul writes, "I urge you therefore, brethren, by the mercies of God, to present your bodies a living and holy sacrifice, acceptable to God, which is your spiritual service [liturgy] of worship" (Rom. 12:1). This begins our act of self-giving to the Lord.

Second, we are to bring God our praise. We are to sing to him. We are to make a joyful noise. We are to offer shouts of victory. God is the great King, and he deserves our accolades. His name is to be exalted. The Old Testament instructs us to "enter His gates with thanksgiving. And His courts with praise. Give thanks to Him; bless His name." (Ps. 100:4). Such admonitions continue in the New Testament: "Through Him [Jesus] then, let us continually offer up a sacrifice of praise to God, that is, the fruit of lips that give thanks to His name" (Heb. 13:15). When we express our gratitude wholeheartedly to God, not fearing what people think, our worship becomes truly self-giving.

Third, we are to give our prayers in intercession. We are to bring our petitions to our mighty King. He wants to hear from us and our requests. He wants to prove to us that he is the living God. God wants us to grow in intimacy with himself. Hebrews 4:16 exhorts us, "Let us therefore draw near with confidence to the throne of grace, that we may receive mercy and may find grace to help in time of need."

Fourth, we are to bring our tithes and offerings to God. The Old Testament clearly demands 10 percent of our income. The prophet Malachi pronounces judgment upon Israel for withholding the tithe and robbing God (Mal. 3:8–10). If 10 percent was required under the law, should we give less under grace? To argue this only barely masks our greed and insecurities. Tithing will test whether our worship is really self-giving and will challenge our materialistic fixes. Self-giving exposes the fear in our hearts that leads us to protect our source of supply. Once we are free to tithe, then we can discover a new release that will fill our hearts with joy.

Fifth, as priests we are to bring God our acts of mercy as a part of our worship. Hebrews 13:16 teaches, "And do not neglect doing good and sharing; for with such sacrifices God is pleased." Our good works are a sign of our love of God: "But whoever has the world's goods, and beholds his brother in need and closes his heart against him, how does the love of God abide in him?" (1 John 3:17). Jesus teaches us in his parable of the day of judgment that as we serve each other with food, drink, hospitality, clothes, and prison visits, we are actually serving him: "Truly I say to you, to the extent that you did it to one of these brothers of Mine, even the least of them, you did it to Me" (Matt. 25:40).

Sixth, self-giving worship includes evangelism. Paul tells the Romans that he is a priest ministering the gospel to the nations. His purpose is to bring them to God's altar, "that my offering of the Gentiles might become acceptable, sanctified by the Holy Spirit" (15:15–16). One day, when we stand before our King, those who have come to Christ through us will be offered by us to him.

Ultimately all of life is worship. All of life is surrender and submission to our mighty King and loving Father. We bring him our bodies as living sacrifices, our praises, our petitions, our money, our good works, and our converts. As we do this, we get out of ourselves and focus on him. All, indeed, is from God and for him and to him.

Self-Giving Preaching

As the Church becomes functional, preaching changes. Sermons must major in solid theology and strong biblical content focused in the cross. Sermons must also be delivered with relational integrity. Ministers no longer are able to hide behind the printed page. Jesus is the one fully functional person who always tells us the truth about himself and the truth about ourselves. We must do the same, especially from the pulpit. This is the only thing that will end hypocrisy and self-righteousness in the Church. When Nathan the prophet brought the truth to David, the chain of sin forged from his adultery with Bathsheba was broken (2 Sam. 12:1–2). David could deceive the nation no longer. No wonder Paul promises the Ephesians that as they speak the truth in love they will grow up into Christ (4:15). Paul continues that they must end the lying that was characteristic of their former manner of life. Deception simply masks sin. Deception is motivated by the fear of being exposed. The truth about God and ourselves, shared selflessly and relationally in preaching, will help us to get free from the shame that binds us.

Preaching honestly from my life has been difficult for me. My strength lies in my historical and theological grasp of the Bible. Sharing myself is another matter. As I have begun to get in touch with my real feelings and learn more about myself, I have been able to put this into my preaching. God is also giving me the freedom not to have everything resolved before I preach.

I encountered this freedom in a startling way several years ago as I listened to John Wimber teach on a Sunday night at the

Anaheim Vineyard, during the summer of 1983. John told his congregation about his recent trip to Chicago. He reported to the two thousand people who had gathered that as he had settled into his hotel room he began to watch a pornographic movie on television. Suddenly, John stopped his narrative. He said, "The Lord just told me not to complete this story." He then asked the congregation to join him in a time of prayer.

The next Sunday night he recalled this incident and explained, "The reason that the Lord made me stop was because I had not told my wife, Carol. Now I can finish the story." As I sat through this I was dumbfounded. I could not imagine any pastor in the country telling his church about watching a pornographic movie. John Wimber displayed a level of honesty from the pulpit that was unknown to me. It was also hard for me to believe that John could be so intimate with the Lord that he could hear God instruct him to stop the sermon until he talked with his wife. My trust in John rose dramatically as I witnessed these events. Others were also influenced. His revelation created an environment in his church where people were able to begin to deal with their own "stuff," because their pastor was dealing with his. This congregation saw their pastor risk vulnerability. He modeled a costly self-giving in preaching. No wonder the Vineyard has become a center for healing and holiness.

Two good questions I've learned to ask as I preach are: How well are my people getting to know God? and How well are they getting to know me? If I am a people pleaser I will tell them what they want to hear, even about myself. I will keep up my false front. I will hide my fear and shame. If I stay in my hiding, however, how can I expect them to come out of their hiding? Self-giving then must be risked from the pulpit if self-giving is to be lived out in the pew.

Evangelism is another aspect of self-giving preaching. As we give up our codependency, the Spirit will lead us to offer salvation to those who are still separated from Christ.

For many years I was afraid to offer an altar call. I felt it to be manipulative, mechanical, and showy. My models (apart from Billy Graham) were poor. Yet when I was honest, I admitted that underneath my intellectual objections lurked the gnawing fear that if I actually asked people to come forward I would end up alone at the front of the sanctuary. The congregation could either conclude that I was a poor preacher or that I had some secret sin in my life that was preventing me from being used by God. For this reason, the most that I did was to ask people to go home and pray alone to receive Christ. For me there would be no "show and tell." I was changed, however, during the Jesus Movement through my friend Verne Bullock.

Verne is a gifted evangelist. Everywhere he goes, he seems to find people who are like ripe fruit ready to be harvested. As I asked him about his freedom to call people to Christ, he assured me that it was all God's work rather than his. Once this concept sunk in, I was set free. If evangelism really is God's work, then my job is to be obedient regardless of the response. As the Lord directs, when I preach the gospel clearly and give the invitation, my work is done. If anyone comes forward, that is up to God. He (rather than my eloquence or emotional punch) opens people's hearts and brings them in.

Once I gave up my pride, my need for approval, and my preoccupation with myself, I was free to fail and free to evangelize. I could begin to put my life on the line for those whom Jesus was already calling.

Self-Giving Community

Self-giving worship and preaching create a self-giving Church. As we have seen, this will be a Church where Christians are learning to love each other as Jesus loves us. In such a Church rugged individualism must go. Each of us must repent of our rebellion, our isolation, and our fear of submitting to each other as the body of Christ. Once this happens, our love for each other will be made manifest in our everyday lives. Such love is not a matter of theology; it is a matter of obedience.

For example, in the New Testament we mature believers are called to pray for the sick. We can obey this instruction today in large gatherings or informal home groups. Such prayer is a self-less, deeply personal ministry that requires time, energy, and sensitivity to the Spirit's guidance. Anyone who risks praying for another's healing must recognize that he or she may not see the results of prayer directly. The format is simple: We begin by interviewing people in order to understand their issues and to know how to pray for them. Then the actual hands on prayer begins. After this, those who have prayed for healing should follow up in order to see what has happened and how to continue to help through prayer.

If we really love people and if we are willing to give ourselves to them, then we will need to learn how to pray effectively for their healing. Jesus restored sight to the blind and cleansed the lepers, not only to establish the presence of God's kingdom, but also because he really loved sick people and had the power to heal them. As we follow in his steps, we will do the same.

Healing through prayer challenges our modern, scientific worldview. If someone has a headache, my first impulse is to send him or her to the medicine cabinet rather than to pray. Since God is the God of creation, as well as redemption, both responses are in order. Too often we rely upon pills and forget prayer. Little by little this is changing. To enter into this ministry of healing, we need to be convinced that healing prayer was not merely for Jesus and the apostles. We need to believe that God continues to care about our sick bodies and damaged emotions. We need to believe that God can break any supernatural bondages that entangle us. We need to believe that healing prayer works.

Dr. David Lewis, a British anthropologist, reviewed the results of 1,890 questionnaires (a 76.5 percent response) that were returned after a healing conference by John Wimber in

Harrogate, England, in the autumn of 1986. Three categories of prayer were analyzed: physical healing, inner or spiritual/emotional healing, and deliverance from demonic influences. Francis MacNutt noted, "Dr. Lewis wisely allowed for five possibilities: 1) *total* healing, 2) a *great deal* of healing, 3) a *fair amount* of healing, 4) a *little* healing, 5) *no apparent* healing."[2] The results amply demonstrated the effect of a self-giving community.

In the area of physical healing, 621 people received prayer for 867 instances of need.[3] As they were prayed for, over 50 percent were clearly touched by God, and for over 50 percent of these, their healing or improvement was permanent. When people simply get together in the context of faith to pray for each other, the results are impressive.

In the area of inner healing or spiritual/emotional healing, some 748 received prayer.[4] Almost 80 percent were clearly touched by God, and most of them experienced lasting help. The biblical writer James was right. If we confess our sins to one another and pray for one another we will be healed.

The most remarkable healings came in the area of deliverance from the influence of evil spirits. Only 104 people were prayed for in this way, but of them 68 percent received a total healing or great improvement, while 17.5 percent received moderate improvement and only 14.5 percent received little or no improvement. What we learn from this study is that Jesus' authority over the devil is released as we command the demons to depart in his name. They cannot stand before him, and they know it.

Praying for the sick is a part of our self-giving service to people. As Bob Jones says, healing provides "signs and wonders" for the nonbeliever, and, at the same time, it is the children's bread, our regular diet in the body of Christ. Often the most loving thing we can do for people is to pray for them.

When we pray about major diseases, such as terminal cancer, we will often need a sustained period of time for prayer rather than just a "one shot" session on a Sunday morning. Francis MacNutt calls this extended prayer, "soaking prayer." Soaking prayer is like spiritual radiation therapy. Many people with physical diseases also need inner healing if they are to be permanently cured. We must pray not only for cancer patients' tumors but also for their repressed anger and emotional denial, which depresses their immune systems. Thus, for them, soaking prayer is necessary.

While I have called praying for the sick a part of the self-giving ministry of Jesus, I must admit that those who do the praying receive much in return. A group from our church prayed for a lawyer with cancer for over a year. As they met weekly, supporting his medical care, he received Christ, became a student of the Bible, saw his cancer go into temporary remission, and experienced much inner healing. At the same time, the group became bonded to him and his wife in remarkable ways.

Ministry to the sick is only one obvious (and neglected) example of self-giving love within the body of Christ. As Jesus cared for the full range of human need, so must we. Like the good Samaritan, our self-giving communities will reach out in active love far beyond the confines of our local congregations. We will agree with John Wesley, who said "the whole world is my parish."

While a self-giving community must be filled with love, it must also be illumined with truth. Alcoholics Anonymous says that we are only as sick as our secrets. So many of us are sick because these secrets keep us living double lives. No wonder more people seek and find healing on a psychiatrist's couch than in most churches. As we have already seen, many Christians are afraid to reveal the pain inside. We are certain that if we do, we will be judged and rejected. Religion without the Spirit suffers under the law and is filled with pride and self-justification. In my experience, people who live in fear of judgment and rejection also harbor a secret self-condemnation. They are their own worst critics. Yet often they hide their fears behind a shield of self-righteousness. They become like porcupines that will stick anyone who comes near. This leaves them bound in endless loneliness.

The only way to break out of self-righteous deception is to tell and live the truth. Then, as John promises, we will walk in the light as God is in the light and have fellowship with one another. This is possible because the blood of Jesus cleanses us from all sin (1 John 1:7). Once when commenting on this promise, my friend Dick Anderson asked the congregation to imagine being in a thick, dark forest with a sunlit clearing in the center. All those present are hiding behind trees in the darkness. Jesus, however, stands in the clearing and calls us to come into the light. This is a fearful moment. We must risk leaving our safety zones. The Lord, however, comes and individually takes us by the hand and leads each of us out. As we enter the clearing, we discover that we are no longer alone, there is a great company walking in the light with us. This, indeed, is a powerful image of an authentic, self-giving fellowship.

In the light we discover that others share our sins and are in need of forgiveness and healing. We no longer live in the illusion that we are "terminally unique." In my church, as we have begun actively to pray for people to be healed, we have found that more and more come to us with a score of disorders: sexual abuse, compulsive masturbation, bulimia, anorexia, and addiction to pornography. People have found an atmosphere of love and trust where they can reveal their sins and wounds. Then as they repent and are healed, the very things that once bound them are now transformed and used for God's purposes. For example, a woman who was a victim of incest and has received healing through prayer has become incredibly effective in praying for those who experienced similar childhood violations. She not only understands the confusion of loving a parent who is an abuser, she also knows how to pray for others out of her own pain and healing. This illustrates the fulfillment of

Paul's incredible promise that as the darkness comes into the light, it becomes light (Eph. 5:14). This is a miracle of God.

When God tells us the truth, he never puts us under condemnation, but he may bring conviction that will lead us to repentance, forgiveness, cleansing, and restoration. Jesus has much more for us than an endless cycle of sin and forgiveness. He wants to restore our fallen humanity and make us like himself. Jesus wants us to be in full fellowship with him and each other.

Along with loving and speaking the truth to each other, a self-giving community will release God's power for the benefit of others. Faith, surrender, and our own growing wholeness keep us from becoming compulsive as we face the sea of need around us. Out of our intimacy with Jesus we will learn that the need doesn't call, but the Lord does. Jesus will call us to the needs he wants us to address. We can also learn to spot the people who have come to absorb our time and take us away from what God really wants us to do. Practicing honesty and honing the ability to lovingly confront people will help us to not be simply carried along by other's agendas for us.

As we expend ourselves for those to whom we are called, we learn the paradox of grace. We work hard. We give ourselves away. Like Paul we "labor"; we strive "according to His power, which mightily works within me" (Col. 1:29).

As our healing continues we will find the freedom to renounce our rights as Jesus did. We have every right to be angry with people who have hurt us. We are free to reject their destructive behaviors. But a time will come when we must surrender these rights for the sake of the Gospel. We are called to forgive our enemies. We learn that abusers abuse because they were abused. We also see the image of God, hidden behind the contorted masks worn by abusive people. This hidden image is what Christ wants to recreate and restore.

A self-giving community of love, truth, and power must disciple Jesus' followers. We must be willing to let people into our lives without fearing what they may discover. We can't hide behind clerical collars, black robes, or Bibles. Ministers especially must be careful not to use their authority to circumvent intimacy or to deny their own attachments and addictions. A radical change in priorities is what leads Christians to seek God's face in prayer. In real prayer we not only speak, we are spoken to. We must learn to listen. For example, after being fired from my previous church, I spent several months alone. I grieved over the loss of hundreds of relationships. My depression later lifted as Nancy Hunt, a dear friend, prayed for me. But I still was unsure of my future. As I sat in the quiet day after day, I began to cry out, "Lord, what do you want me to do?" One special morning as I repeated this into the darkness several times, my final petition trailed off, "Lord, what do you want . . . ?" In the stillness, the words came back crystal clear, "I want you." Here was God's answer. God didn't simply want me to *do* something, He wanted *me*! He wanted me with all of my loneliness and confusion about the future. He wanted me with all of my sin and failure. He wanted me to be intimate with him and to bow before his throne. The direction my future would take would become clearer as I spent time with my "Abba" just as children learn by sitting on their daddys' laps.

The intimacy we have with God is what allows us to be authentic with others. As our wounds are healed we can become "wounded healers" as we invest ourselves in the lives of others. Our Lord invested himself in a circle of friends. He lived with them and they "caught" his ministry by following him around Galilee. In like manner, people will catch our ministry by being with us. I recall when I first saw John Wimber pray for the sick. Drawn by his example, I asked him how I could do the same. John's reply was simple: "Just keep showing up." He knew that I would believe in God's power to heal and learn how he prayed for people by observation. As we see God's power at work, our hearts will be drawn to ministry.

A self-giving community is a group of Christians who also suffer for Jesus' sake. The cross was Jesus' ultimate act of self-giving. Jesus called us to share his sufferings in the world. As we have seen, this means dying to our false self, our sin nature, our pride, our religiousness, and our addictive attachments. But as Paul teaches, the Christian life is both justification and sanctification, crisis and process. Paul did not die with Christ once and for all. Paul continually bore the dying of Jesus (not just the death of Jesus) in his body (2 Cor. 4:10–12). This meant that he died daily (1 Corinthians 15:31). Paul's sufferings were *physical.* Paul was bounced around the Mediterranean world, homeless, hungry, and hounded by his enemies. He was stoned, beaten, and shipwrecked. His sufferings were also *emotional:* he was filled with frustration and agony until Christ was fully formed in the lives of his converts. Paul knew loneliness, sorrow, and the threat of death itself, and yet he went on for the sake of others. Finally, Paul's sufferings were *spiritual,* as the apostle bore the pain of living in a lost world with his eyes open. He experienced constant harassment from the devil. The thorn in his flesh never left him. He experienced both his own weakness and the power of God. And with it, unlike much of the modern Church filled with self-righteousness and religious pride, he can clearly distinguish between his limitations and that which God does through him (1 Cor. 2:3–5).

The life that Paul lived is also the life for us. Like Paul, the members of the self-giving Church must endure physical stress. Most Christians who live in the Second and Third Worlds suffer the same malnutrition and diseases as their fellow citizens. Despite the break-up of the Soviet Empire, many continue to experience persecution and martyrdom. The self-giving Church is subject to emotional stress. Our hearts are broken again and again. The self-giving Church also experiences spiritual stress. We are not retired veterans. We are an army, laying siege to the very gates of hell (Matt. 16:18).

New Life

Jesus was a *receiver.* He received the Father's presence and purpose and so do we as we remain in intimate communion with God. Jesus was also a *giver.* He restored our fallen humanity, forgave our sins, healed our diseases, drove out our demons, and united us to himself and to each other. By his example and by his Spirit he now teaches us how to live fearlessly, freely, and selflessly. This is what it means for us to be in communion with Jesus, the one fully functional person.

As Jesus heals our being wound by his presence, our generational and environmental sins begin to be broken. We become willing to let go of our addictive attachments. As a result, our new humanity emerges out of bold worship, honest witness, Spirit-empowered works, and authentic relationships. Through our new humanity we can shine with the glory of Jesus' presence and become givers like him. This is the hope of the Church. This is the hope of the world.

Conclusion

Go Tell the Church

. . .

In my former church a couple vanished for several weeks from a large adult Sunday school class. Finally, some concerned friends went to their house and were met at the door by the wife. After an exchange of pleasantries, she revealed that her husband was suicidal and had admitted himself to the psychiatric ward of a local hospital. While his wife appreciated the visit, as it ended, she gravely asked, "Please don't tell the church. It would be too embarrassing, too humiliating." Rather than crying out, "Please tell the church, we need prayer and love now as never before," she silenced these friends out of her fear of exposure and judgment. She was more afraid of the self-righteousness that plagued the church than she was of suffering alone.

A new Church, however, is emerging: a Church that welcomes suffering people just as they are. The new Church lives grace, grace, grace. In it addictions to substances, processes, and people are confronted. Codependency is admitted rather than admired. The new Church is found where God will fill the hole in the soul with himself. This is a Church where generational sin is broken, environmental sin is overcome, and personal sin is forgiven. This is a Church where the false self dies and abandonment ends. The new Church is where our being wound is healed.

The new Church is centered in the fearless, free, and self-giving Jesus, where Jesus' agenda for ministry is pursued, love is unconditional, and human control is surrendered. This is a Church under the control of the Spirit.

This is a Church where all are addicts and are taking responsibility for their recovery, where a fresh, real commitment is born. This is a Church where sin is inventoried, confessed, and forgiven, where people are healed and delivered and amends are made. This is a Church where prayer and meditation prosper.

This church is filled with praise, prayer, and the gifts of the Spirit. Here the cross is preached and tithes are paid.

This is a Church where love is extended, accountability is demanded, and relationships prosper, where the lost are found, the poor are clothed, and the hungry are fed. This is a Church that is taking the good news to the nations.

Where this Church is emerging, people who are caught in crisis, bound in shame, fearful of judgment, addicted and despairing can cry out, "Go tell the Church." Such a Church will respond by offering a flood of grace, water for the thirsty, bread for the hungry, refuge for the abused, deliverance for the addict, and love for all.

The new Church is Jesus' Church. He designed it and called it into being. It is the choir for his worship. It is the family for his love. It is the weapon for his warfare. It is the Church—militant in its suffering. It is the Church—triumphant in his return.

Are you weary? Fed up? Famished? Faint-hearted? Helpless? Hopeless? Lonely? Empty? Lost? Trapped?

Go tell the Church.

Notes

Chapter 1   Naming Addiction in the Church

1. For documentation see Anne Wilson Schaef, *When Society Becomes an Addict* (San Francisco: Harper & Row, 1987), 15; Herbert L. Gravitz and Julie D. Bowden, *Recovery: A Guide for Adult Children of Alcoholics* (New York: Simon & Shuster, 1985), 4; Anne Wilson Schaef, *Co-Dependence Misunderstood—Mistreated* (San Francisco: Harper & Row, 1986), 4; John Bradshaw, *Bradshaw on the Family* (Deerfield Beach, FL: Health Communications, 1988), 6.

2. Gerald May, *Addiction and Grace* (San Francisco: Harper & Row, 1988), 3–4.

3. "When a Pastor Turns Seducer," *Newsweek*, 28 Aug. 1989, 48.

4. May, *Addiction and Grace*, 3.

5. Stanton Peele, *Love and Addiction* (New York: New American Library, 1975), 17.

6. Alice Miller, *For Your Own Good* (New York: Farrar, Straus & Giroux, 1984), ix.

7. Ibid., 7.

8. Ibid., 87.

9. May, *Addiction and Grace*, 26–28. May adds to the three Cs that an addiction will produce two withdrawal symptoms. First, a stress reaction when the body is deprived of the addicting object. Second, a backlash reaction: Symptoms that are the exact opposite of the addictive behavior itself will appear. Thus withdrawal from stimulants creates lethargy. Also an addiction will perpetuate itself through self-deception or mind games and result in a loss of will power. An honest test for an addiction is— "simply go ahead and stop it."

10. Schaef, *When Society Becomes an Addict,* 18.

Chapter 2   Getting to the Root of Our Addictions

1. Bob Dylan, *Lyrics, 1962–1985* (New York: Knopf, 1985), 443.

2. Gershin Kaufman, cited in John Bradshaw, *Bradshaw on the Family* (Deerfield Beach, FL: Health Communications), 2.

3. Ibid.

4. Gerald May, *Addiction and Grace* (San Francisco: Harper & Row, 1988), 99–100.

Chapter 3   Grace, Grace, Grace

1. Rich Buhler, *Love: No Strings Attached* (Nashville: Thomas Nelson, 1987), 25ff.

Chapter 4   At Home With the Father

1. Joachim Jeremias, *New Testament Theology* (New York: Scribners, 1971), 61–68.

2. J. B. Phillips, *The New Testament in Modern English* (New York: Macmillan, 1959), 405.

3. Helmut Thielicke, *The Waiting Father* (New York: Harper & Row, 1959), 22.

4. Gerald May, *Addiction and Grace* (San Francisco: Harper & Row, 1988), 96.

Chapter 5   Living With the Fearless Jesus

1. Gerald May, *Addiction and Grace* (San Francisco: Harper & Row, 1988), 17.

2. Alice Miller, *For Your Own Good* (New York: Farrar, Straus & Giroux, 1984), xi.

3. Ibid., 85.

Chapter 6   Living With the Free Jesus

1. C. S. Lewis, *Mere Christianity* (New York: Macmillan, 1953), 40.

2. Dietrich Bonhoeffer, *The Cost of Discipleship* (New York: Macmillan, 1963), 137–138.

Chapter 7   Living With the Self-Giving Jesus

1. Melody Beattie, *Codependent No More* (New York: Harper/Hazelden, 1987), 33.

2. Cited in D. Martyn Lloyd-Jones, *Joy Unspeakable* (Eastbourne, England: Kingsway, 1984), 62.

3. Dwight L. Moody, *Secret Power* (Ventura, CA: Regal Books, 1987), 17.

Chapter 8   Giving Up Fear

1. Allan Eister, "Oxford Group Movement," in *Twentieth Century Encyclopedia of Religious Knowledge,* ed. Lefferts Loetscher (Grand Rapids, MI: Baker Book House, 1955), 828–829.

2. *Alcoholics Anonymous*, 3rd ed. (New York: Alcoholics Anonymous World Services, 1976), 59.

3. Gerald May, *Addiction and Grace* (New York: Harper & Row, 1988), 96.

4. *Alcoholics Anonymous,* 59.

5. May, *Addiction and Grace,* 94.

6. *Alcoholics Anonymous,* 59.

7. May, *Addiction and Grace,* 3–4.

Chapter 9   Getting Free

1. *Alcoholics Anonymous,* 3rd ed. (New York: Alcoholics Anonymous World Services, 1976), 59.

2. Ibid., 59.

3. Alice Miller, *For Your Own Good* (New York: Farrar, Straus & Giroux, 1984), 7.

4. John Bradshaw, *Homecoming* (New York: Bantam Books, 1990), xi.

5. *Alcoholics Anonymous,* 59.

6. Ibid., 59.

Chapter 10   Giving Myself Away

1. *Alcoholics Anonymous,* 3rd ed. (New York: Alcoholics Anonymous World Services, 1976), 59.

2. Ibid., 59.

3. Ibid., 59.

4. Ibid., 59.

5. Michael Cassiday, *Bursting the Wineskins* (London: Hodder and Stoughton, 1983), 117–122.

6. *Alcoholics Anonymous,* 60.

7. Russell Chandler, "'Customer' Poll Shapes a Church," *Los Angeles Times,* 11 Dec. 1989, 29A.

8. Ibid., 28A

9. Ibid., 30A.

Chapter 11   A Fearless Church

1. Howard Snyder, *The Problem of Wineskins* (Downers Grove, IL: Inter-Varsity Press, 1975), 23. We accept here the "fear of God," which is our awe and reverence before him, especially as we are confronted with his holiness and power. This fear does not drive us from him; rather, it draws us to him. We are allured by his majesty. Out of this fear we want to submit ourselves to him and worship him. This fear then defines the limits of our humanity, as we recognize that God is God. This is a healthy rather than neurotic fear.

2. Cited in John Randolph Taylor, *God Loves Like That!* (Richmond, VA: John Knox Press, 1962), 46. Since we are all guilty of generational sin, environmental sin, and personal sin, if we want justice from God he would send us all right to hell. We all deserve condemnation. What is surprising is that any of us receive salvation.

3. Justin Martyr, "Apology I,13.4," in Martin Hengel, *Crucifixion* (Philadelphia: Fortress Press, 1977), 1.

4. Martin Hengel, *The Son of God* (Philadelphia: Fortress Press, 1976), 91.

5. Ibid., 1.

6. Cited in Hengel, *Crucifixion,* 30–31.

7. Cited in Taylor, *God Loves Like That!,* 55.

8. Ernest Becker, *The Denial of Death* (New York: The Free Press, 1973), ix.

9. Snyder, *The Problem of Wineskins,* 140–143.

10. For a balanced introduction to the ministry of the Holy Spirit and the spiritual gifts, see Michael Green, *I Believe in the Holy Spirit* (London: Hodder and Stoughton, 1985).

Chapter 12   A Freeing Church

1. Alice Miller, *For Your Own Good* (New York: Farrar, Straus & Giroux, 1984), 6.

2. Ibid., 90. Miller writes that the child-rearing methods of the nineteenth-century pedagogue Daniel Gottlob Moritz-Schreber "were based on the need to stifle certain parts of one's own self. What Schreber, like so many parents, tries to stamp out in his children is what he fears in himself. . . ."

3. This term, coined by C. Peter Wagner, defines the current movement of the Holy Spirit that is found outside of the Pentecostal and Charismatic movements.

Chapter 13   A Self-Giving Church

1. The Hebrew word is *shakah,* the Greek *proskuneo.*

2. Francis McNutt, "From Francis," in *Christian Healing Ministries, Inc.,* Vol. 4, Iss. 1, January, 1990, 1.

3. Ibid., 2.

4. Ibid., 2.